U0520371

孫正義：事業家の精神

愿景

孙正义一生的精进哲学

汉英双语版

［日］井上笃夫 — 著
陈述斌　马社林 — 译

中信出版集团｜北京

图书在版编目（CIP）数据

愿景：孙正义一生的精进哲学：汉英对照／（日）井上笃夫著；陈述斌，马社林译. -- 北京：中信出版社，2021.10
ISBN 978-7-5217-3401-0

Ⅰ.①愿… Ⅱ.①井…②陈…③马… Ⅲ.①孙正义－传记－汉、英 Ⅳ.①K833.135.38

中国版本图书馆 CIP 数据核字（2021）第 149646 号

SON MASAYOSHI JIGYOKA NO SEISHIN written by Atsuo Inoue
Copyright © 2019 by Atsuo Inoue.
All rights reserved.
Originally published in Japan by Nikkei Business Publications, Inc.
Simplified Chinese translation rights arranged with Nikkei Business Publications, Inc. through Bardon-Chinese Media Agency

愿景：孙正义一生的精进哲学
著者：　　[日] 井上笃夫
译者：　　陈述斌　马社林
出版发行：中信出版集团股份有限公司
（北京市朝阳区惠新东街甲 4 号富盛大厦 2 座　邮编　100029）
承印者：　宝蕾元仁浩（天津）印刷有限公司

开本：880mm×1230mm　1/32　　印张：11　　字数：200 千字
版次：2021 年 10 月第 1 版　　　 印次：2021 年 10 月第 1 次印刷
京权图字：01-2021-5564　　　　 书号：ISBN 978-7-5217-3401-0
定价：65.00 元

版权所有·侵权必究
如有印刷、装订问题，本公司负责调换。
服务热线：400-600-8099
投稿邮箱：author@citicpub.com

目 录

序言　成就一番事业 —— 致所有创业者、
企业家及生意人　// V

第一章
美好人生

众人脸上绽放的笑容就是我快乐的源泉 // 003
作为一名企业家，我未有大成，
　但雄心壮志不减 // 006
谢谢你，逆境 // 009

第二章
要做个天才

孙正义不会永远活着，但"正义"会 // 015
智慧的大脑也是一种力量 // 018
不要一味地效仿他人 // 021

以坂本龙马为偶像 // 024

好！很好！大快人心！// 028

我下定决心要发明一种发明方法 // 031

百万美元的合同 // 036

**第三章
自我锤炼**

我只是不甘居于人后 // 043

恩人感谢日 // 046

成功不能仅靠聪明 // 052

只要有七成胜算，那就全力冲刺 // 055

冥思苦想 // 060

**第四章
战略与筹划**

企业管理的核心是管控黄色区域 // 067

人生就像玩《超级玛丽》游戏 // 072

我之所以出离愤怒，是因为我对成功的
　渴望无人能及 // 077

若员工考虑一步，则企业家应该考虑
　三百步 // 080

做好多手准备 // 084

风险与危险 // 088

"一流攻守群" // 091

第五章
言行一致

我将永远恪守承诺 // 099

我的发际线没有后移，只不过是我在
　不断前行 // 102

我宁愿做硅谷 // 105

放飞自我，自由飞翔！// 109

第六章
技术进化论

洞悉时代潮流 // 115

寻找下一个马云 // 117

传感器、三叶虫和寒武纪大爆发 // 119

期盼奇点 // 121

第七章 献给将与人工智能共存的人类

要像年轻的绝地武士一样 // 127

人工智能将重新定义所有行业 // 130

误差,时差 // 132

"说大话"心态 // 135

我也许会后悔,但决不退缩 // 137

为工作而狂 // 141

后记 // 145

附:孙正义大事年谱 // 149

英文部分 // 155

参考文献 // 319

序 言

成就一番事业

——致所有创业者、企业家及生意人

本书旨在把日本著名企业家孙正义先生在商业生涯中的心态特征和思维习惯分享给大家,若各位读者能有所获,并将其与自身的生活融会贯通,则吾心甚慰。

动笔前,本人就对本书的目标读者群有了清晰的思路:它是写给那些雄心勃勃的创业者、企业家和生意人的。过去的30年间,我和孙正义先生有过许多次面谈,对他非常了解,在本书中,我将主要按时间顺序,采用传记的形式向大家一一介绍他那些最具代表性的言行。

通过本书,我希望能回答一个近年来引起全世界广泛关注的问题——孙正义是谁?

我相信,孙正义先生的商业思想不仅对日本民众有益,而且对世界范围内所有的年轻人和创业者都有益。

孙正义先生一直将自己定位为企业家。那么，在他眼中，什么是企业家，什么是创业者，二者的区别又有哪些呢？

多年前，孙正义先生就对此做过明确的陈述和界定，他说："创业者开疆拓土，生意人披荆斩棘，而企业家则成就事业。"

开始写本书时，我又一次问了他这个问题：创业者、生意人和企业家之间究竟有什么不同？2019年10月18日，我收到了他的回信，我们主要谈论了一些关于创业者的话题。而我就以这次采访作为本书的开篇，以下就是我与孙正义先生在采访过程中的谈话内容。

***

问：您曾经说过："创业者开疆拓土，生意人披荆斩棘，而企业家则成就事业。"今天，您能不能更加具体地谈一谈这三者的区别到底是什么？

答：从某种程度上讲，创业者必须有一种近似疯狂的拼劲，他们需要想别人不敢想的事情，开辟别人未曾涉足的路。也就是说，在我的观念中，真正的创业者就是那些既不循规蹈矩，也不随波逐流的人。

问：不少创业者就是因为自己离经叛道的观点或者行为而

麻烦缠身，甚至被所在的公司扫地出门。您会觉得这些人太过疯狂了吗？

答：他们确实可以被称为"疯狂"。不过，更准确地说，他们只不过是和周遭的人比起来显得……有些不同而已。

一般情况下，人们不会一直保持着这种"疯狂"的状态，当他们有所建树、功成名就时，这种劲头就会逐渐消失。

问：也就是说，在那个阶段，他们还不是真正的企业家？

答：对。但是，这种作为创业者的阶段是非常重要的。

以史蒂夫·乔布斯为例。他年轻时就因为这种"疯狂"被赶出了苹果公司。但之后他回归苹果公司，并且带领公司取得了震惊世界的辉煌成就。这一刻，一位"疯狂"的创业者就蜕变成了真正的企业家。当然，他之所以能够实现这样的转变，是因为在经历过一些挫折和困苦之后，认清了自己真正想要追求的事业。

创业者表面上看起来很"疯狂"：他们说话"胡言乱语"，行为"离经叛道"，人们并不是一开始就能理解他们的所作所为。

问：那倒是。否则，创业者就无法真正做到开疆拓土了。

答：是的，我认为，这类和人们普遍思维方式完全不同的观点必定是不会被轻易理解的。很多事情正是如此，但凡是我们想方设法让人接受的观点往往很难得到他人的认同和理解。这就像某一种另类艺术或者摇滚音乐一样,最开始往往得不到人们的理解。

我之所以欣赏创业者,是因为他们所展现的才华就像艺术家进行创作一样。他们的行为催生了一些从未有过的事物,这就是创造力。我非常看重这一点,也十分尊重创业者。

截至2019年11月6日,我们通过日本软银愿景基金投资了90家初创企业。从某种程度上说,这些创业者都会表现得有些疯狂,他们这群人能够让自己的初创企业发展到市值超过10亿美元,也就是我们所说的独角兽级别。即使在我们称之为"疯狂"的所有创业者中,他们也称得上是真正的商界骄子。

可以这样认为,不能达到上述成就的创业者,是在没有创造出超过10亿美元市值前便停下了奔腾的脚步。他们也曾是奔马,但停歇让他们无法长出翅膀,而只有长出翅膀的骏马才能飞翔,才能变为独角兽,才是真正优秀的创业者。

问:是不是成功的创业者,只看他们有没有"翅膀"?

答:是的,就看"翅膀"。因为他们不仅要"奔跑跳跃",还要在"天空中飞翔"。当然,区分"马"和"独角兽"的标准便是看企业市值能否超过10亿美元。是否冲破10亿美元的大关决定你能否拥有"翅膀"。尚未达到这个标准的创业者可能也会奋力向上弹跳,但他们不可能"飞上天空"。他们只是没有"翅膀"的"马"啊!(大笑)这便是区分你是"马"还是"独角兽"的根本标准——有没有"翅膀"。

很多总裁都自诩为创业者,我就想问他们这样一个问题:"你们有'翅膀'吗?"换句话说,对他们而言,现状可能只是一次短暂的跳跃,他们的客户数量还没有达到百万以上的水平。

如果一位创业者的企业用户数量达到100万以上,企业市值往往能接近10亿美元。在达到这一水平时,他们便会获得这100万个客户的青睐,这又会给他们带来新的财富价值,那么,企业的市值便会达到10亿美元。

如果企业用户量小于这个数字,那是决然不行的。你可能短暂地在行业中名列前茅,但也可能会被超越。或者说,在还没等到规模变得非常大之时,企业就有可能走上了下坡路,甚至慢慢被淘汰。

对我而言,这些创业者都是雄心勃勃、满怀理想的人。他们有热情,但是缺乏技巧。也就是说,这些创业者不能如愿地让客户理解他们。他们有想法、乐于挑战,但最终没能大有收获。他们不能在"天空中飞翔",最终也不能变成"独角兽"。

创业者不应简单地模仿他人，他们热情地创造新事物，勇敢地接受新挑战。他们开创事业，绝不拘泥于规则和现有的事物，他们做的是真正的"开拓性创业"。这样，他们便能产生全新的观念，这正是一位创业者该有的作为。

但是，我认为，在冲破10亿美元企业市值，突破百万用户大关之前，他们都不能算真正意义上的创业者。他们可能在非常努力地发展新事业，但是还算不上真正地"飞"起来了。他们还达不到长出"翅膀"的水平。这时，他仍然是一匹"马"，就和其他"马"一样。

我想支持这种能够为数百万用户创造价值、有可持续发展潜力的企业，于是，我创立了"愿景基金"。

可持续发展意味着有"翅膀"，能够连续不停地"飞翔"。要是没有"翅膀"，你就只能原地起跳，然后又落回地面。跳跃和飞翔的区别在于能否长时间待在天上。没有翅膀，你也可以跳跃，但是只有长出翅膀，你才能够飞行。拥有百万用户、10亿美元企业市值，企业才能可持续发展，才能在"长出翅膀"之后变成一只"独角兽"。

愿景基金的作用就是挖掘独角兽企业，培养它们、支持它们。这样它们才能变得更大更强，继续飞翔。

目前，还没有一家投资集团专注于投资这种独角兽企业。

全球大概有5 000家风险投资公司正在寻找和培养自己理想的公司，他们认为只有符合以上要求的理想公司才可能是下一头巨型独角兽。但是，这些风投公司大都是在做无用功，他们投资的公司根本还没有达到能成为独角兽的水平。

相比之下，要是培养那些已经达到独角兽水平的企业，比如愿景基金，就会有不同的发现，它们甚至在资金投入方面都有所差别。

问：在对它们的投资力度方面会存在巨大差异吗？

答：是的，对"马"的创业投入肯定与"独角兽"存在很大的差异。

给"马"投资一两千万美元的"干草"和"胡萝卜"就足够了；而在天空飞翔的"独角兽"是不吃"胡萝卜"的，它们吃的可是"彩虹"，它们还需要在天空中飞翔着寻找"彩虹"。一只"独角兽"需要投资逾10亿美元的"彩虹"，所以如果想投资一百只，所需的资金规模就高达1 000亿美元。

所以，我创立愿景基金的时候就知道需要1 000亿美元的启动资金。从一开始我就明确地了解到了这一点，但是，当我提出这个观点时，现软银集团负责人，时任软银集团战略财务部主管的拉杰夫·米斯拉和其他人都认为我一定是疯了。

问：即使是拉杰夫先生也觉得您当时的想法完全不可

思议？

答：是的，最开始拉杰夫认为少则20亿美元，多则300亿美元就足够了。他觉得，投资这么多已经是极限了。

那时候，世界上没有一家基金公司的投资额度达到这个水平。最高的投资额可能为5亿~10亿美元。两年前，我们了解到整个硅谷范围内最大基金的资金规模也只有10亿美元左右。

由此，在我提出成立1 000亿美元资金规模的愿景基金后，很多家基金公司也试图效仿我们，临时准备投入更多的资金，加大投资力度。然而，对任何一家基金公司来说，突然拿出如此巨额的资金都不是一件轻而易举的事情。

这些基金公司大多都有三四十年的历史，但就算是最好、资历最老的风投公司也很难一下子拿出如此巨额的资金。当然，它们也没有这种完全创新的想法，因为，它们并没有想过要把资金完全集中投到独角兽企业上。

问：所以，您认为要缩小投资范围，就要减少投资目标的数量吗？

答：每个人追求的目标各不相同。如果你努力地想要捕捉一只海狸或梭鱼，思维方式、准备程度与捕捉一头鲸的情况一定截然相反，投入规模自然也不一样。追求的目标不一样，未来的规划不一样，努力的方向不一样，志向也就不一样。

我认为，在众多初创企业创业者中，这些独角兽才是真正意义上的初创企业创业者。

而且，那些尚未达到独角兽水平的创业者还在不断地努力着。

问：如您所说，许多初创企业的创业者现在还只是努力向"独角兽"转变的"马"，但是，他们之中只有一小部分能变为"独角兽"，成为有所建树的企业家，是这样吗？

答：目前，大多数风投公司倾向于走"广而浅"的路线，大范围撒网投资可能成为"独角兽"的公司。我想投资的并不是这种公司，而是已经成长为"独角兽"的初创企业，它们已经明确知道如何成为行业标杆，并且开始"吃彩虹"了，它们已经做好了一骑绝尘的准备，"独角兽"早已长出"双翼"，准备起飞了！

问：所以，您能看出哪些"马"未来会飞，是吗？

答：如果它们有能力飞，或者已经飞起来了，我就能看到它们的翅膀。

我们只投资能看见"翅膀"的公司，看着它们成为"独角兽"，并开始"飞翔"。

当然，这些独角兽企业以非常高的水平成就并保持着它们的事业。更确切地说，它们能够上市，并且它们的企业价值可以发展到300亿~1 000亿美元不等。只有符合上面这两个条件才能算得上是真正的事业，才能产生真正的企业家。而且，我认为最低标准应该在300亿美元左右，一旦一家企业的市值突破这个数字、用户数量超过100万，并且开始在世界范围内提供服务，它就能称得上是真正有成就的企业。所拥有的企业能达到上述规模，并且还在不断创新的人，我们就可以称其为企业家。

换句话说，虽然企业达到了上述两个要求，但还要有能力持续发展。大多数情况下，这些企业家就是公司的创始者。

然后，企业将被传递给第二代、第三代、第四代、第五代……如果后来的接班人有能力保持原有的成果，并创造新的成绩，那么这些人就可以被称为企业家。他们往往头脑冷静，拥有专门的技能和知识。而一名卓越的企业家能够自信而周全地解决他所遇到的各种问题。

企业家不需要前面所说的那股疯劲，他们只需要拥有时刻保持冷静的心智、突出的职业技能、精深的专业知识。拥有了这些综合素养，他们便可以在面对任何未知的情形时审时度势、探索前行。"疯狂"状态，对他们来说是没有用的。

但是独角兽企业的创业者确实需要一定程度的疯狂劲头，

那是他们前进的动力和创造力的源头。只有这种近似疯狂的特质才能让他们有所突破。

我认为，乔布斯就是这样一个不可思议的人。

因为"疯狂"，他被赶出公司，但也正是这种"疯狂"，让他克服了层层困难，解决了重重危机，重回苹果公司，把一个几近破产的公司变成了世界排名第一的巨头。我认为，乔布斯正是在经历过这些挫折后才获得了如此卓越的成就。

问：另外，我还想问您一个问题。您认为，在未来的企业中，企业家需要做些什么，才能成为一名成功的领导者？哪怕是初创企业的创业者，也得在一个规模相当大的团队中展现自己的领导力，用独角兽般独特的思维方式行事，而很多事情仅仅依靠创造力是不可能完成的。那么请问，您认为在AI（人工智能）时代成为一名企业领袖，需要做到哪些方面？

答：我认为人工智能技术将会创造一个完全不同、充满竞争的世界。

工业革命前后，影响企业成功与否的因素发生了巨大变化。

工业革命之前，成为一名大地主的关键就是拥有大量的土地和劳动力。每一寸土地都有它的价值，如果拥有的土地不够多，你就无法成为一位真正的拥有土地的农场主。

问：是的，没有土地就无法获得事业上的成功。

答：工业革命之后，情况就不同了。要是一个人不了解工业体系，不懂新科技，也不知道怎么使用新科技，那就无法成为一名企业家。除了这些，你还必须拥有另外一样创业利器——资金。对，你需要的就是资金。

而到了互联网时代，你甚至都不需要资金，只要拥有专业技能和知识就可以创业。如果你懂互联网，还知道如何使用互联网，那就能成为GAFA（谷歌、亚马逊、脸书、苹果）——四大互联网巨头中的一员，开启你的创业生涯。所以，一个全新的时代到来了。

互联网时代广义上被包含在信息革命时期内。这个时期，互联网创造的价值总量呈现爆炸式增长。在这个时代到来之前，是PC（个人计算机）时代，我们也可以将它看成互联网时代的先导。更早之前便是大型电子计算机时代。

大型电子计算机时代的英雄不可能在PC时代也是英雄，PC时代也不可能产生互联网时代的英雄。

至于互联网时代的英雄会不会成为人工智能时代的英雄……我相信一个截然相反、充满竞争的世界即将到来。

为了成为人工智能时代的英雄，你首先必须了解人工智能的技术要素、技术知识，并掌握相关的专业技能，才能确保有机会接触真正懂得应用人工智能技术的工程师。

你还要知道要运用人工智能技术做什么。

目前，互联网时代已经给人们广泛定义的两大产业带来了革命性的变化。

第一是广告业。公司建立了大量网页和新媒体，极大地冲击了报纸、杂志、电视和收音机等传统媒体形式。

第二是零售业。像亚马逊、阿里巴巴之类的公司利用互联网——更确切地说是通过电商——改变了零售业。消费者通过互联网轻轻一点就能获得自己想要的信息并购买商品。

在互联网时代之前，邮购依靠电子通信技术存在。而在更早之前，人们就开始通过报纸、电视购物之类的媒介进行邮购了。网上购物更加经济、便捷，还能使企业为潜在客户提供更多信息。电商本质上是指互联网成为邮购的主要媒介。

广告业和零售业是两个明显被互联网"取代"的产业。客观而言，广告业占美国国内生产总值（GDP）的1%，零售业占6%——总共占了7%（该数据由日本软银集团据美国经济分析局文件估算得出）。

不仅是广告业和零售业，人工智能时代的来临也会影响所有的行业。人们可以运用人工智能为医疗界带来新的药物治疗方法，也可以将人工智能技术运用到酒店、办公场所和交通运输领域。像优步和滴滴之类的企业就改变了我们的出行方式。

金融科技领域也有新的变化，人工智能改变了银行业、证券业和保险业的发展方向。

我想说的是，人工智能不单单会影响广告业，或者零售业。不仅在美国，在世界范围内，人工智能都可以在另外93%的GDP中作为一种全新且强大的武器。而且在此过程中，它会给各行各业带来革命。

而当这一刻来临之时，只知道使用因特网或者在键盘上打字是远远不够的。你还得对每个行业有自己的理解。

问：对极了。我们不仅要明白人工智能技术正在改变世界，还要了解那些被人工智能改变的产业。

答：以医疗领域为例，在你用人工智能技术对医疗产业进行变革之前，就要对这个产业进行深入了解。要改变医疗产业或者是交通运输业，可不仅仅是建立网站那么简单。你需要一位司机为你开车，需要一位真实存在的司机在现实中的马路上驾车行驶。

如果你想要研究出新的药物疗法，就要和正在进行实验的实验室建立紧密联系。互联网时代，几乎所有酒店都要和电商相结合，接受网站预订，向来十分注重酒店管理模式革新的印度OYO酒店，也正在彻底改革酒店管理方式。在这个时代，你不仅需要对人工智能的相关技术进行知识储备，也需要对特定的行业有深刻的理解，要有能力管理一个复合型团队，有能力用垂直的商业模式管理工作人员。

所以你不仅需要有实操技能、管理才能和新技术方面的专业技能，还需要有能力管理更大的团队，不仅是人文社科方面的员工、整天对着电脑工作的科研工作者，还有体力工作者和外贸业务员。

你可能以为这个时代是一个知识导向型时代，但事实并非如此。你要想具有竞争力，就必须拥有某一行业的管理技能，能够在该行业中运用人工智能技术。

这需要更加专业的技能，一个人成为将人工智能技术运用到所有行业的专家是不太现实的，能成为一位精通如何将人工智能技术运用到某一特定行业的专家就很了不起了。如果你想用人工智能技术分析血液和DNA（脱氧核糖核酸），以筛查早期癌症，你就需要花费大量的时间研究肿瘤学。此外，还需要有管理技巧，你要能够直接管理医院、医生和患者，并把这项服务销售给这三者。这不是IT（信息技术）公司仅凭一己之力就能做成的事情。

所以，在这个新时代，每一个行业都会涌现出新的英雄。在人工智能时代谈论人工智能公司，人们的第一反应便是你在说一个研发人工智能技术的公司。他们往往会认为人工智能公司就是自己在新闻里看到的那种公司，如某人工智能机器人打败了某将棋①、象棋或围棋②专业选手。

但这只是把人工智能技术作为一种工具，和音频图像识别技术毫无区别，只是在贩卖工具而已，而一家工具经销商能做成的事情显然十分有限。

互联网时代初期也是如此，受欢迎的都是那些把互联网作为工具销售的公司。

石油时代到来的时候，也发生了同样的事情。首先取得成功的是工具店，他们售卖开采石油的钻机，然而，石油时代最后的赢家是用钻机获得石油的人。而到了互联网时代，赢家是那些利用互联网为人们提供长期服务的公司，你看，亚马逊和阿里巴巴就没有发明互联网。那些能够最大限度利用互联网，发挥互联网最大效能，解决服务业长期需求的公司的规模呈爆炸式扩张。

---

① 日本将棋：日本传统棋盘游戏，和国际象棋相似。在2012—2017年日本举办的将棋赛事中，专业将棋选手对阵电脑软件。许多专业将棋选手败给了电脑软件，被媒体广泛报道。

② 围棋：被称作非常复杂的智力游戏，也被认为很难有一款围棋电脑软件能打败人类。但在2017年，美国谷歌公司开发的"阿尔法围棋"打败了世界知名的中国围棋选手，这一事件受到媒体广泛报道。

同样，如果我们把人工智能技术作为一种工具加以利用，就会有很庞大的市场需求。而能用100亿日元、1 000亿日元投资于挖掘市场潜力、实现产业革命的公司，未来会发展壮大，成为时代的英雄。

所以，因为虚拟现实技术而轰动一时的公司，在一开始就会进行大肆宣传。

问：但是它们不会一直"在空中飞行"。

答：确实如此。

问：它们没有可持续发展的可能性吗？

答：正如我所说，它们只是"工具店"。它们也许只是一家拥有虚拟现实技术的"工具店"，但是它们能为这个世界做出什么贡献呢？有了它们，物价会下降吗？可以提供更多贷款吗？

虚拟现实技术本身并不能使物价下降，或者创造出更好的处理方法。问题的根本在于你如何使用这项技术，用这项技术为人们提供何种服务，或者是想进入哪个大市场。能做到这些的公司会让人觉得不可思议，但是如果你做的只是售卖技术、贩卖工具，那你就是一个不折不扣的工具销售者。

我们的第一家公司是销售PC软件的。起初，有关编程语言的软件销量十分高。提供编程语言，如BASIC语言和FORTRAN语言，以及开发工具和研发环境的公司，曾经都非常受欢迎。但如今，这些公司中的大多数已经不复存在了。换句话说，它们是"工具店"，很难向大规模、可持续发展的公司转变。

问：您的意思是，要想经营一家有可持续发展潜力的公司，市场选择很重要，对吗？但是您为什么不提坚持不懈的毅力也是一个重要的因素呢？行动了，就要一直坚持下去；向前进，就要一直向前进，永不言弃。我记得您曾经说过这样的话："烧吧！烧吧！烧吧！燃尽我所有的精力！"

还有一件让我印象深刻的事情，您一直说："我们已经进入了AI时代。"某一次，您询问周围的人："你真的相信AI时代已经到来了吗？你确信这一点吗？"您问了身边很多人这类问题，一部分人表示自己也有点不确定。在那之后，他们才开始后悔当初的犹豫不决。我认为，正是这些因素对事情的发展起到了关键作用，如果一个人愿意采取行动，并为此坚持不懈，无论发生什么都专心致志，那么，他们就一定能够取得成功，是这样吗？

答：很多人能提出有创意的想法。但是大多数人都会吹嘘自己，夸夸其谈，比如说："这个主意是我第一个想到的。"（笑）是的，很多人都会炫耀自己是第一个想到某个观点的人，当然，这也是一件很难的事情，而且做第一个提出某个想法的人也十分有必要。要是没有这些人,我们就不可能看到新的领域出现。

但是,做第一个想到某个想法的人……和第一家生产电视机的公司不一样,第一家生产电视机的公司现在已经独占鳌头了。

最后,如果你只是一股脑儿地去实现梦想,你就不可能一直是赢家。

现实就是你要处理各种残酷、棘手的事情。现实世界从来都没有"容易"二字,不会总是晴天,还有阴天、雨天,甚至是暴风雨。

你要做的就是不要放弃,不要丧失希望,克服各种难题和困境。而区别在于……你是否能在暴风雨中一直前进,不找借口退却;是否能够咬紧牙关,冲破障碍,继续飞行;是否能够持续飞行,永不停歇。你如何才能做到这些呢?

我认为答案是热爱。疯狂又强烈的热爱。这属于情感投资。

问:怎么理解"疯狂的热爱""情感投资"呢?

答:你要在暴风雨中保持疯狂,继续前行,步履不停,即使困难重重,九死一生。

问:您曾经说过,想要成功,人需要变得更"疯狂"一些,是吗?

答：是的，你需要变成一个近似"疯狂"的人。

问：您觉得一些人还不够"疯狂"，是吗？

答：确实。人们一般都会认为遇到了暴风雨天气就不应该继续飞行，而是要停下休息。如果有人说下暴雨的时候要出去钓鱼或者飞行，这听起来很不可思议。所以，所有人都会选择一种相对安逸的方法生活，于是，他们选择了休息。

实际上，选择在暴雨中出行就一定会遇到一些常人遇不到的事情。

问：如果他们确实有所行动，会遇到危险吗？

答：我认为这正是机会。

问：哦！您看到的是事情的另一面。

答：假设有一百匹马，只有一匹马想要飞上天空，那么这匹马需要做的就是在其他马停歇的时候，疯狂地奔跑，只有凭着这股疯劲不停地狂跑，它才会在这个过程中长出翅膀。

问：您认为，根本原因是人们还不够"疯狂"吗？

答：是的，确实是这样。

无论是清醒的时候还是休息的时候，我们都要不停地思考这一点，并仔细想清楚。一个人要对"疯狂"的状态抱有极度的热情，要有抱着这些想法进入梦乡的热情，否则，你很难在竞争中让对手望尘莫及。

我的意思是，生活没有那么容易，你不疯狂地工作，生活自然不会随随便便回馈你，让你在任何事情上有所成就。

这的确很困难。要长出翅膀在天空中飞翔本来就不是件容易的事情。

你必须不停奔跑，像发疯一样奔跑，无论是遭遇暴风雨，还是其他一切困难和阻碍，你都要越过眼前的悬崖，疯狂地向前冲，跳过下一个峭壁。集中你所有的精力完成一次次跳跃，不停地跃向空中，在这个过程中，你可能会一次次掉落下来，但是你要一遍又一遍地尝试，纵然一次又一次地落回地面……哪怕每一次都回到同一个地方，你还是要再次全力冲刺，只为到达另一个悬崖的最高处。如果你坚持这样做，那么最后，一定会长出"翅膀"。

没有这种情感投入，没有这种志向抱负，没有这种几近疯狂的努力，你不可能长出"翅膀"。

结语

"疯狂"的初创企业创业者需要这种"疯狂的热爱"，只有这样才能长出"翅膀"，成长为企业家。他们需要更加"疯狂"，更加认真地对待关于疯狂状态这件事。感谢您给初创企业创业者和全体想成为初创企业创业者的人带来的分享和启示。

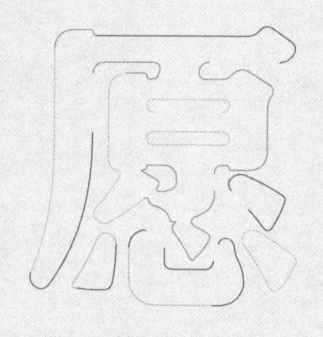

第一章
美好人生

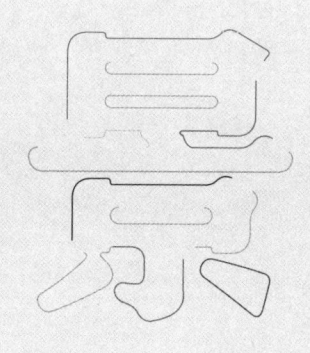

众人脸上绽放的笑容就是我快乐的源泉

2019年4月25日,孙正义在"软银职业生涯"活动现场给新一批有意愿加入软银集团的求职者做主题演讲。这项活动是日本最有影响力的职场活动之一。孙先生时年61岁,他站在讲台上侃侃而谈,听众是那些将承担起21世纪商界未来的年轻人。

"人生仅此一次,我不能把时间和精力全部用来赚钱。"

因为25岁时的亲身经历,孙正义有了这样的深切体会。那是他创办日本软银公司(现软银集团)的第二年,正是那一年,他因为严重的肝炎必须住院接受治疗。当时,医生已经明确告诉他,他的时日无多,仅剩5年时间可活。而彼时,他才刚刚成立软银公司，他的第二个孩子也才刚刚出生。

他只能哭。在医院里独自一人时，他悲伤地哭了起来，他不禁问自己：我为了什么而拼命工作？工作的意义是什么？我为什么要为了参加公司的管理层会议，甚至偷偷地溜出医院？我又是为什么因为医生不允许我工作而冲他们大吼大叫？

是为了钱吗？但命没了，一个人要钱又有什么用呢？

是为了声名显赫，还是为了荣华富贵？然而这些并不是他的终极追求。

冷静思考后，他终于意识到自己最大的追求是：给他人带来欢乐，让他们幸福，让孩子们脸上洋溢着灿烂的笑容。直到那时，埋在他灵魂深处的情感涌了出来。"我意识到世间最珍贵的东西莫过于女儿的笑容，这就是我想活下去的原因。我想看着家人幸福的笑容，我想每天都能够工作，看见每位员工的笑容、每个顾客的笑容。不仅是他们，还有身边无数人的笑容。"

"我常常这样想，如果在世界的另一端也有人使用软银公司提供的服务，那么他们知不知道公司的名字、知不知道这些服务的创造者是我们并不重要。我只希望他们在使用服务的过程中，因为这些服务本身而微笑着轻轻地说声'谢谢'，哪怕他们不知道具体应该感谢谁。"孙正义先生这样讲道。

幸运的是,孙先生最终战胜了疾病,得以痊愈出院,回到了正常的生活轨道上,但他仍怀揣着那份藏于心底最深处的感情。

28年后,也就是2011年3月11日,日本东部发生大地震。每天新闻里都会播放一个个小镇被海啸淹没的镜头,灾难似乎没有尽头。这样的情形让人感到心急如焚。

第二天,也就是3月12日下午,福岛第一核电站的1号反应堆发生氢气爆炸。同月22日,孙正义带着盖革计数器(一种专门探测电离辐射,如α粒子、β粒子、γ射线和X射线等强度的计数仪器)赶到了福岛的一处避难所。在那里,同样的想法一次又一次撞击着他的心灵。

在这场导致超过1.5万人死亡的自然灾害面前,人类无能为力。孙正义不禁自问,他为之奉献一生的信息革命是否能够拯救深陷这场灾难的人呢?

如果不能,那么信息革命的意义何在?孙先生陷入了长时间的思想斗争之中,为此寝食难安,甚至好几次在开会的时候,突然开始抽泣,全然不顾他人的看法和眼光。

那段日子,日本各地民众挣扎于水深火热之中,而孙先生的日子也过得非常煎熬。

然而，他最终得出了自己的结论："即便信息革命解决不了当下人们的困境，我们仍然需要继续推进这场革命，与之一起向前迈进。"他为什么能得出这样的结论呢？

"于我来说，只是为了自己开心。因为只有看见人们的笑容，我才能感受到真切的幸福。"

他的这种感情一天天强烈。

作为一名企业家，我未有大成，但雄心壮志不减

"作为一名企业家，我觉得自己还是一事无成，但我有达到最终目标的雄心壮志。"2018年8月11日，孙正义在61岁生日时说了这样一句话。

这听起来不像是一位日本家喻户晓的企业家所说的话。

"我曾与一些金融界、政治界的大人物有过面对面的交流。"

他口中的"大人物"指的是世界范围内的一些业界名人。

"但我最钦佩我的父亲。即使现在，我最钦佩的人仍是我的父亲。"

原因非常明确。

"他拥有无可比拟的专注力和竞争意识。"

他的父亲，孙三宪，出生于1936年，是在日朝鲜人，也可

以称这类人为日本的朝鲜族永久居民。为了养家，中学刚毕业，他便开始赚钱谋生。起初，他在母亲的养猪场帮忙，离家以后，他卖过烧酒，做过投资，也取得了成功。他是一位精力充沛的人，热衷于享受生活，并把这些事情做到极致，而且他的成长环境并未阻碍他的发展——他的儿子们是这样评价他的。

19岁时，他便竭尽全力帮助父母盖了一栋豪华的小楼。最终，孙三宪一共开了20家弹球盘（日本一种类似于弹球的赌博游戏）店铺。在那之后，他还提出了拓宽生意范围的想法，并不断扩张生意，成为新锐企业家。他白手起家，养育了四个儿子，次子就是孙正义，四子是孙泰藏。孙泰藏创建的公司投资了许多很有前途的初创企业，他也因此而出名。孙三宪的长子和三子也有各自的生意。

"我觉得我是家中的第1.5代人。"孙正义说，言语中表达了他对父亲的尊重和钦佩之情。他的意思是，虽然他不是继承了父亲事业的第二代人，但他继承了父亲身上许多了不起的品质。

孙三宪常常发自内心地称赞他的儿子们，那便是他给孩子们灌输动力的方式。每当重要时刻，他会对着儿子们喊："天才正义！""天才泰藏！"他相当认真，并发自内心地相信这一点。即使现在孩子们已是成年人了，孙三宪依旧会这样对着他们大喊。

"他真情实意地赞扬我们。如果你以一种鼓励的方式教育孩子,他们会真切地感受到,我父亲是最好的教育家,他对我们既诚实又坦率。"

作为一名居住在日本的朝鲜人,孙三宪说:"你要留下,就得按规矩来,否则没有人会接纳你。"孙三宪坚定的信念贯穿其一生。

孙家四兄弟都在各自的领域取得了成功。然而,一说到商业,他们却异口同声:"没人能与父亲相提并论。"

从创立软银公司开始至今,孙正义每天都会打电话给他的父亲,只是为了听听他的声音。"从公司创立开始,每天都是如此。"孙正义说。

孙父对儿子的公司非常了解,几乎到了无所不知的程度。从孙正义还在福冈市博多区的和音世界工作,到20世纪80年代初在东京创办日本软银公司,孙父都参与其中。那时的公司还在销售计算机软件和使用手册,40年之后,在如今的时代,人工智能开始成为现实。孙父比任何人都关注公司的未来,从1000亿美元的"软银愿景基金",到目前隶属软银的英国主要半导体设计公司ARM有限公司,以及软银的物联网业务,比如人形机器人"派博"(Pepper)的开发。

他的父亲常常这样对他说："经商最有趣的地方就是使人们感到快乐。"孙正义说："我父亲最理解我,也最支持我。"

每当听到父亲的声音,孙正义的信念便会更加坚定。

"我想成为对大家有益的企业家,努力工作,为世人带来幸福。"

这就是父亲的言传身教。

2016年,软银的年度综合净利润突破1万亿日元。

而现今,孙正义还是说着同样的话。

"作为一名企业家,我觉得自己一事无成,但我有达到最终目标的雄心壮志。"

谢谢你,逆境

2019年4月,孙正义在429位软银新员工面前发表了讲话。此时,日本软银电信公司已经成为软银集团的核心公司。

"无论事情的发展多么糟糕,过程多么艰辛,都没有关系。只要你有干劲、有动力,竭尽全力地去奋斗,就会渡过难关。总会有一些时刻,你不得不面临一些工作上的困难。你可以灰心丧气,但你也可以在磨砺中吸取教训,从而让自己变得更加优秀、强大。这取决于你个人,取决于你的思想观念,一切都取决于你自己的行为。逆境会使你更加强大。所以，我很开心能在年轻时遇到逆境。实际上，我甚至想对过往说：'谢谢你，逆境。'"

孙正义说到这些时，脑海中可能已经浮现出日本卓越的军事家山中鹿之介[1]在向月亮祷告时所说的话："请赐我千难万险吧！"山中鹿之介曾深受日本战略家织田信长[2]尊敬，他在历经多次逆境之后，成为一位了不起的军事统帅。

孙正义也曾面临过接踵而来的麻烦，包括他在创立软银公司之后与病魔的斗争。

2004年，他遇到了人生中最大的逆境。软银BB公司[3]发生了大量客户个人信息泄露的事故，人数达451万之多。罪犯伙同软银销售子公司的业务合作伙伴，企图利用客户个人信息进行敲诈勒索，最终被逮捕。孙正义知道，此次事故会威胁到公司的生存。

---

[1] 织田信长同时代的军事统帅，以骁勇著称。
[2] 16世纪（日本）战国时代，日本四分五裂，相互争夺控制权。织田信长是一位致力于民族统一的军事统帅。他还因其革新策略而闻名，包括先于对手将西方火器投入战斗，以及促进商业发展。他是孙正义的榜样之一。
[3] 前公司名，目前已并入软银日本电信公司。

2004年1月19日,孙正义亲自拿起电话报了警。

"我是软银的孙正义。"

这是在孙正义收到员工宫内谦报告后的第三天。刚从海外出差回到日本的孙正义立即针对这个问题专门成立了调查委员会,他们没日没夜地调查了三天,并果断采取了措施。

"我一定能化解这场危机。这是我的职责。"孙正义一直抱着这样的信念。

2月27日,公司举办了新闻发布会。孙正义认为,那个长达两个半小时的记者提问环节并不是最让他饱受折磨的时刻。

"因为我相信人性本善,所以我们没有严格控制别人的质询权。"

他一边表达着公司的反思结果,一边一次又一次地鞠躬致歉。

他保证从今以后会从防患于未然的角度出发经营管理公司。他是这样承诺的,也是这样执行的。

然而,从最初相信人性本善转向相信人性本恶,对孙正义来说,似乎是极其艰难的。于他来说,那天才是人生中最艰难、最痛苦的一天。

多年后的2019年4月,孙正义又一次站在了逆境重生的软银公司的员工面前发表了一次演讲，他的话似乎是说给在场的每一个人听的。

"每个人都有自己无法改变也不需要改变的地方，但也有一些他们不得不改变的地方。例如，你必须珍视人类的本质和激情，保持自我，守护灵魂，尊重并爱护他人。但同时，在知识技能方面，必须每天不断学习、不断进步，而不能安于现状，满足于自己的现有水平。"

企业家的本质就是要不断学习、不断进步，你的努力付出会让你的事业发展得越来越好。日复一日，只要你保持着自己一贯的精气神，即使面临再多的艰难困苦，它也只会让你变得更加强大。这正是孙正义常说的：

"谢谢你，逆境。"

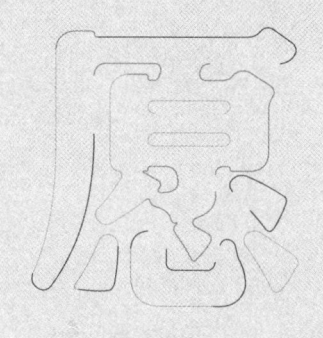

第二章
要做个天才

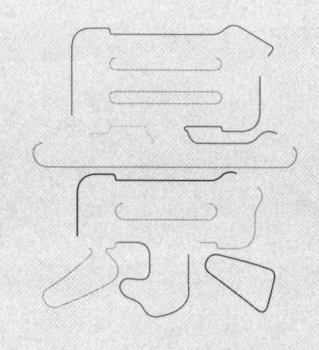

孙正义不会永远活着，但"正义"会

"我生来就有一种信念感。"

孙正义 1957 年 8 月 11 日出生于日本佐贺县鸟栖市，他的父亲叫孙三宪，母亲叫李玉子，孙正义在家里四兄弟中排行老二。他家当时所在的地区是一个朝鲜族聚居地，他们是在 20 世纪 40 年代中期之前就陆续搬迁到这里安家落户的。算起来，孙正义是第三代朝鲜裔日本人，当然，他已经是日本的朝鲜裔永久居民了。

虽然不确定，但据说孙家的祖先早前是从中国迁移到朝鲜的。其家族史上才俊辈出、人丁兴旺，不仅出过将军、学者，还出过许多有影响力的人物，这些都被清楚地记录在孙家的族谱中。

在孙正义祖父那一代，他们全家从现在的韩国大邱市迁至日本九州地区。

孙正义的父亲孙三宪最开始是靠打鱼和卖猪肉维持生计的，后来又改行销售日本烧酒。之后，他做起了弹球盘生意，几经周折，还开过饭店，从事过房地产生意，多年的经商给孙家带来了较为殷实的家底。

然而，在孙正义出生时，孙家的经济情况并不是特别好。

孙正义曾不止一次地对他父亲说："真的感谢您给我起了一个这么好的名字，您确实给了我一个再好不过的名字啊！"

从下面的故事中我们就能看出孙正义为什么这样说。据他父亲回忆：一次，在和儿子说话的时候，他在态度上表现得有些冷淡，没想到，当时还是小孩的孙正义竟然径直走到了父亲面前，大声地说出了下面的话，且语气颇为不忿。

"父亲，您为什么对我这么冷淡？您为什么这样对我？"孙父回忆道："当孙正义遇到觉得不公正的事情时，总是喜欢以这样的语气去追问，从小他便是这样了。大概是从上小学开始，他就是这副样子了，你甚至会觉得这孩子有些令人生畏，那段时间，他总是觉得自己是对的，执拗极了。"

当孙正义还小的时候，他曾有一段时间因家庭背景而被周围的人嘲笑,甚至瞧不起。

"嘿,朝鲜佬!"一些孩子经常会冲他大喊,还朝他扔石头。一次,他被一块石头砸中了后脑勺,鲜血直流。

"那时候,我非常痛苦,甚至想过一死了之。即使现在,在下雨天的时候,我偶尔似乎还能感受到当时的那种痛苦。"

那种痛苦在他心灵上留下了深深的烙印,形成了难以抹去的伤疤。

但孙正义并没有因此对伤害他的人怀恨在心。

他的祖母曾教导他:"不要把仇恨放在内心。"

19岁时,孙正义为自己制定了一份清晰、详尽的人生规划——50年人生规划。

20多岁时,要声名鹊起。

30多岁时,要积累资本。

40多岁时,要全力一搏。

50多岁时,要成就大业。

60多岁时,要主动让贤。

"我从未改变过这份规划,现在我也是按照这份规划生活的。"

"孙正义不会永远活着,但'正义'会。"

智慧的大脑也是一种力量

"父亲是一个非常健谈,而且能绘声绘色地给别人讲故事的人。"谈起自己的父亲,孙正义的弟弟孙泰藏这样说道。

"父亲似乎有各种讲不完的荒诞离奇、刺激惊险的故事。"

孙三宪的故事大多数以某位英雄的事迹为中心,而且故事的结构也大同小异:"主人公往往会主动热情地帮助他人;主人公总是主动寻找挑战并克服它们,解决问题,就像民间传说里聪明的一休哥那样。"

比如,有一次,一头牛连同套着的拖车一起掉进了路边的沟渠中,牛被困在下面,大声地哀号着,很多人围了过来,但一时都无计可施。恰好此时孙三宪路过,他也想要帮忙把牛拉出沟渠,结果发现办不到,牛就卧在原地,一动不动。他思考了一会儿,就想到了一个好办法。他先是跑回家拿了一瓶自家卖的烧酒,举起酒瓶一股脑儿地灌进了牛嘴里,让牛喝了下去,随后,他又在附近捡了一根铁棍,把它烧到炽热,发出"嘶嘶"的声音。接着,不可思议的一幕发生了,他用这根烧得滚烫的铁棍结结实实地烙在了这头"醉牛"的臀部。瞬间的疼痛加上酒劲,使这头牛大叫着蹿出了沟渠,问题就这样被解决了。

这个故事是孙泰藏讲述的。你似乎能从他讲述故事时流露出的神情中感受到孙氏家族以前居住的村庄的那种热烈、快乐的氛围。村子里的人会把剩菜剩饭收集起来喂养牲畜，大家勤俭持家，以苦为乐。而孙三宪则有一种不畏艰难、锲而不舍的精神。

孙正义上小学的时候，孙三宪开了一家有山间小屋风格的咖啡店。

孙泰藏说："有一天，我父亲在每天上下班经过的路边看到了一间十分简陋的棚屋上写着'此房出租'的字样。我父亲是那种总是四处寻找商机的人，所以当他看到'出租'字样时，就忍不住想去看看，更何况这处房子就在他每天上下班经过的路上，十分便利。"

这间老棚屋所在的位置并不是很好，毫无疑问，很多人不可能愿意在这样的地方做生意。但是孙三宪还是每天都留意这间房子的出租情况——"此房出租"……

日子就这么一天一天地过去了，整整一年后，这间棚屋还没有人来租住。

又过了半年，有一天，孙三宪路过那间棚屋，发现有一位老妇人正在打扫屋子。

于是，孙三宪问道："您是房东吗？"

"是的。"老妇人一边回答，一边抱怨地说道，"没有人愿意租这个地段的房子。我不知道该怎么办了。我们以前是农民，现在年纪大了，没办法干活了，入不敷出。如果有人能租下这里就好了，那真是帮了我们一个大忙。"

得知这个情况后，孙三宪想都没想就说："我租！我租！"

他租下这里后，心里就开始盘算应该用这里来做些什么。

他想，这是一间老棚屋，那不妨把它改造成一家山间小屋式的咖啡馆。为了节省成本，他发动全家人上山捡石头和木头，将这间老棚屋变成了一间真正的山间小屋。

孙三宪总是称那时还在上小学的孙正义为"天才正义"。那是他对孙正义的专称，而且他从心底里认为自己的儿子是一个天才。他和孙正义说话的语气，就好像他们俩是工作搭档。

"孙正义，你的想法是什么呢？你觉得我们怎样才能将这家店铺开得红红火火呢？说来听听。"

孙正义当即就说："赠品。我们可以赠送一些免费的咖啡券吸引顾客。"

父亲果然采纳了他的建议，孙正义十分擅长绘画，他在每张免费的咖啡券上画了插图。结果，咖啡店因此大受欢迎，成了附近人们经常光顾的场所。

日子就这样一天天过着，他们的父亲喜欢动脑筋，一直想着在不同的事情上获得成功。他和自己的生意伙伴——他的天才儿子孙正义一起为孙氏家族开创致富之路。

2001年，孙正义已经长大成人，开始供职于互联网服务公司雅虎。为了增加一项新服务的业务量，公司做出了一个重大决定，免费给用户提供宽带网线。我们不难看出，这个决定就反映出孙三宪对孙正义商业思想的影响。

"只要大脑没爆炸，就要不停地思考。"

这是孙正义从他父亲那里学到的，也是他一直挂在嘴边的一句话。

孙正义说："你的灵感和想法是无限的，永不枯竭，要不停地思考，不断酝酿新想法。如何才能尽可能高效地利用你的思想和头脑呢？"

"船到桥头自然直。你越是觉得'只能这样了''太难了'，越是想不到办法去解决问题。"

"智慧的大脑也是一种力量。"

孙正义像运动员锻炼肌肉力量一样锻炼自己的大脑，这种习惯是由他父亲用各种激动人心的故事逐渐培养形成的。

不要一味地效仿他人

在孙泰藏还是个小学生的时候，有一天，他放学后回到家时,刚好父亲孙三宪也在家。

父亲说:"你回来了。"随后又问他:"今天在学校学了什么?"

他回答:"今天我学了分数除法,要先把分数倒过来,然后使它们相乘。"

孙三宪点头说:"我知道了。"

随后,又语重心长地说了这样一句话:"学校老师教的东西不要全信。"

孙泰藏当时对此十分震惊,问道:"啊?我不应该听老师的话?您为什么这样说呢?"

他对父亲的话感到十分困惑,但孙三宪却坚定地说:"学校的老师也会撒谎,他们的话不要全信。"

孙泰藏在成为一名父亲之后,才慢慢理解孙三宪那句话里蕴藏的真正含义。他父亲想要表达的是:每个人都要学会独立思考,要具备这样的能力,而这就是批判性思维的重要性。

多年以后,孙泰藏似乎已经忘了父亲说过的那些话:"学校老师教的东西不要全信""学校老师会撒谎"……但在他初为人父的时候,那些话突然又浮现在他的脑海中。

"父亲常常语出惊人,说一些充满了智慧和哲理的话。"

孙泰藏说,他的哥哥孙正义也总是妙语连珠,这或许就是从父亲那里遗传的。

孙三宪经常对他的儿子们说的另一句话便是"不要一味地效仿他人"。

比如,有一次,父亲问了孙泰藏一个问题:"如果有人找到你,对你说他们想要辞去公司的工作,开一家日本拉面馆,你会怎么做?你问他们,他们是否会做拉面,他们说不会,之前也从来没有做过拉面生意,但是他们很爱拉面,觉得公司的工作太枯燥了,他们就想尝试一下。如果他们询问你的意见,你会怎么回答?"

孙泰藏的回答是:"辞职我支持,但是我建议他们应该先去一家老牌拉面馆接受培训,在那里先学习一段时间。你觉得这个主意如何?"他认为这是一个合理的建议,总体阐明了自己想要表达的内容。一位志向高远的拉面师傅可以在那里学好基本技能,再自创一些新颖的拉面手法,然后就可以开一家属于自己的拉面馆了。这是一个可行的计划。但是在孙家,正确答案却截然相反:

"先把那些豚骨炖了!"

当然,在那个阶段,你并没有接受过任何烹饪培训,肉汤可能做得十分糟糕,但是如果你不断地练习,一遍一遍地炖煮那些豚骨,掌握好放盐的量或者改变其他调料的分量,并不断尝试新的配方,那么这配方便是你的原创了。

如果按照这种方式进行,你的生意不可能只比那些老牌拉面馆好一点。反之,你去一家新开业的拉面馆进行培训,学习既有的知识,这样就不可能比那些老牌拉面馆做得更好。而若你只是比同行好一点,顾客可能就会直接去那些老牌拉面馆用餐,而不需要光顾你这里了。

所以,孙家总结出了"不要效仿他人"的道理。

孙泰藏的哥哥孙正义说:"效仿他人,是无法超越他人的。"这是孙家核心思想的体现。

以坂本龙马为偶像

孙正义非常崇拜日本明治维新志士坂本龙马[①]。坂本龙马是日本历史上的一位杰出人物,他致力于推动日本明治维新改革,为19世纪日本革命运动的发展做出了巨大贡献,留下了

---

① 坂本龙马(1836—1867年)是日本历史上一位有影响力的武士,致力于江户幕府向明治政府的政治过渡。坂本龙马建立了日本第一家贸易公司——龟山社中(海援队的前身)。32岁被暗杀。坂本龙马的生平被日本著名作家司马辽太郎(1923—1996年)写进了历史小说《坂本龙马第一部》。

浓墨重彩的一笔。

孙正义把一张和坂本龙马真人等比例的写真挂在了办公室的会议桌前，这样，他就能时刻看到自己的偶像，在无形之中时刻督促自己不断前行。

孙正义经常用一种假想的情景来鞭策自己，比如坂本龙马就站在自己对面，对他说："你依旧很渺小，还不够优秀。"于是，他每一天都会感到坂本龙马在激励着他更努力地工作。

孙正义15岁时读了司马辽太郎的《坂本龙马第一部》，这本书对他的影响非常大，甚至改变了他的人生观。

孙正义在坂本龙马的人生经历中似乎看到了自己的影子，这让他深受鼓舞。

坂本龙马出身商人世家，最开始只是地位卑微的下级武士。他小时候十分胆小，经常受到邻里其他小孩的戏弄和欺负。孙正义也是如此，他是商人之子，童年时期也曾因出身饱受他人欺凌，同样的经历让他觉得坂本龙马非常亲切，这似乎拉近了他们之间的距离。

不久之后，孙正义就像坂本龙马当年脱离土佐藩籍一样，毅然从高中辍学，独自远走美国。要知道，按照当时日本的律法，坂本龙马脱藩可是犯了重罪的，不但本人要被处死，还会牵连家族，做出这样的决定需要很大的勇气。虽然孙正义做出这个决定的后果不像自己偶像的那样凶险，但同样需要魄力。

坂本龙马和日本第一个商业协会性质的组织——龟山社中，也就是后来的贸易组织海援队取得了紧密联系。作为日本明治维新的领导人物，虽然坂本龙马后来遇刺身亡，未能看到新政府的建立，但就算他能活着，也不会在新政府寻求一官半职。

"比起成为日本政府的一员，坂本龙马更想推动贸易组织海援队走向全球。他的雄心壮志远超我们的想象，他想与全世界热衷于改革现状的人合作，布局日本的国家未来。"

孙正义志在追随海援队的脚步，追随自己的雄心壮志，致力于将软银集团经营成一家全球性公司。他也在不同的场合反复表达过自己的这一追求。

每当孙正义遇到困难时，总会这样思考：如果坂本龙马遇到这种情况，他会怎么做？

这就是为什么他说："我一想到自己在这个年纪还一事无成，就会感到恐慌，我对自己还有很多不满意的地方。"

任何时候，只要是孙正义在办公室开会，他的身边总会放着一把木剑。

任何时候，当他感到激动，或者愤怒时，就会郑重地拿起那把木剑，用力地做出劈杀的动作。

这个时候，所有的经理和员工都会不由地发出惊呼、赞叹。

孙正义中学时曾在当地的剑术馆接受过北辰一刀流派的正规训练，他的剑术可是一点儿都不马虎，绝对是真才实学。坂本龙马也曾学习过这种剑术。孙正义说，他是从司马辽太郎所写的坂本龙马传记中获得这些信息的，这让他对坂本龙马的崇拜之情更盛了。

"对我来说，最大的快乐便是在我生命的最后一刻，可以感慨道：'我的一生是多么波澜壮阔啊！'"

如果必须要用一个词来形容坂本龙马和他的一生，这个词肯定是"波澜壮阔"。对于怎样活得洒脱，孙正义有很多看法。

胸怀大志，忍辱负重，历经大起大落，奋力拼搏，无问西东，不欺人，守诚信，不断地反省自己是否独立自强，活得真实诚信。

他认为，一个人必须这样活着。

只有这样，当生命走到尽头，闭上眼的那一刻，我们才能有资格说："我的一生是多么波澜壮阔啊！"

孙正义一直在努力工作，为的也是有那么一刻可以这样回顾自己的一生。

"我要追随坂本龙马，活出波澜壮阔的人生。"

好！很好！大快人心！

并不伟岸的身材，典型的亚洲人面孔，略带娃娃脸，孙正义就是这样一位面相和善、颇有魅力的人。

2000年11月，孙正义在美国拉斯维加斯生活。

当时正是互联网泡沫破灭时期，我坐在米高梅大酒店的一个房间里等待着孙正义的秘书通知我去采访他。

没过多久，我收到了第一封邮件，几番沟通之后，我终于收到了"孙正义先生马上会离开会议室"的信息。我立刻起身赶去会议室外。

我看到了这样的场景：孙正义和几名员工走在拉斯维加斯一家大酒店宽敞明亮的走廊上，孙先生走在最前面，身后跟着几个身材高大、体形健硕的外国人，反衬之下，他看起来就像是个小孩。这个场景实在有点奇怪。

但是当我看到孙正义自信地和那些身材高大的员工一起走来时，内心最直观的感受却是：这个人多酷啊！

很快，就像电影里的场景一样，员工悄然退下，我和孙正义先生并肩继续往前走去。

孙正义先开口了。

"好，好极了，真是大快人心。无论什么时候，在美国，我都很兴奋。"

尽管在他16岁时已经被日本九州的一所著名学校——久留米大学附属高中录取了，但他还是决定从日本辍学，去美国学习。他是在暑假结束后做出这个决定的，之所以会做出这个决定，首先是因为他有过在国外为期四周的英语学习经历，那时候，他看到了当地绮丽的美景——广阔的蓝天和加利福尼亚州美不胜收的风光。

"大海多么辽阔，天空多么蔚蓝啊！"孙正义不禁发出了这样的感慨。

在这之前，孙正义也曾为自己的未来担心、惆怅过，作为一个朝鲜裔日本永久居民，他知道从日本的高中毕业再在日本读大学，对他来说并不是一个明朗的未来。

但是当他看到加利福尼亚的天空时，所有的担忧都烟消云散了。

孙正义就读于旧金山南部戴利城的塞拉蒙提公立高中。他成绩优秀，跳级并通过了高中水平考试，三周后就从高中毕业，进入了圣名大学学习。他学习的时候就像个疯子，近乎痴狂。

他自称"学习狂魔"，把自己的学习时间安排得非常紧凑。他在两个钢柜的顶部放了一块从家具店买到的大木板，制作了一张巨大的书桌。然后，他把课本、参考书和字典等都摆在了桌上，这样，他就不需要浪费哪怕一秒钟的时间去书架边拿书。他还对自己的裤兜做了改动，给裤子缝上了两个大口袋，可以同时将几支笔、尺子还有计算器等学习用具都放进去，这样他就可以随时拿到自己想要的东西。他的大背包里塞满了各种课本，哪怕是吃饭的时候，他都至少有一只眼睛是盯着参考书和笔记本的。他心里想：总有一天，我可以全神贯注地吃饭，而不用看这么多书。

但也正因为如此拼搏，他才有资格转学到选拔更为严格的加利福尼亚大学伯克利分校。

孙正义经常说："有没有人和我一样用功？如果你认为你是，请举手。"他说这话的时候，是在开玩笑的，但事实的确如此。

在美国上学时，有一天，孙正义在超市排队结账时正在翻阅一本杂志，突然灵光乍现，那种感觉让他兴奋地几乎晕了过去。

"真是一种美妙到让人难以置信的感觉！"

多年后，孙正义再回想起那一刻时，他说，当时因为激动，自己的眼泪"就像被打开的水龙头里的水一样流了下来"。

他看的那本科学杂志上面的几何图案是 Intel 8080 电脑芯

片。他将那张彩页从杂志上剪了下来,放进文件夹中,随身携带。

"即使到现在,我仍然记得自己当时深受鼓舞,那股突如其来的、强烈的灵感深深地影响了我后来的生活方式。"

"工作就是为了尽情享受这种灵感。我想做的就是分享这种灵感。这难道不是一个人能做的最幸福的事情吗?"

他说:"那种感觉就像是,我和好朋友结伴去山上探险时所感受到的那种兴奋。"

现在已年过六旬的孙正义常说:"我生命的青春光彩依然灿烂夺目。"

"当我迎接新事物的时候,我所感受到的那种灵感带给我的快感一直没变。"

从这样一个无拘无束的、诚实的人身上迸发出的灵感是一种强大的动力——一种能使其他人行动起来的力量。

我下定决心要发明一种发明方法

计算机先驱艾伦·凯曾经说过:"预测未来最好的方法,就是去创造未来。"

刚转学到加利福尼亚大学伯克利分校不久的孙正义就已经

是一位发明家了。

孙正义的成绩非常优异，他的数学、物理学、计算机科学和经济学等科目的成绩都位列全班前 5%，他许多科目的成绩甚至排名全班第一。

孙正义清楚地知道他的主要任务就是学习，所以他不做任何兼职。

然而，他觉得自己不应该完全依靠补贴维持日常生活的开销。

他每天会抽出大约 5 分钟时间做一些与学习无关的事情。

他甚至想是否能每天只工作 5 分钟，每个月就能挣到 100 万日元。

听到这个想法后，朋友们禁不住嘲笑他说："你是疯了吧？"

当时才 20 岁的孙正义反复思考后得出了一个结论，能让他达到这个赚钱目标的工作就是搞发明创造。于是，他每天都会发明一件东西。

他会准备一个被称为"创意库"的笔记本，然后设置 5 分钟的倒计时。在这 5 分钟之内，他会集中自己的思绪，挖空心思地构想一个具有创造性的主意，如果 5 分钟内仍没有想出一个创意，他就会放弃。

结果是，他在每天的 5 分钟内想出了各种各样的创意。例如，用塑料泡沫制成的马桶座圈垫；可以不弄脏手的吃比萨工具；专门为有视觉障碍的人提供的交通信号灯，等等。

随着时间的推移，他似乎才思枯竭了，在越来越多的日子里他没有更多的创意了。现在该怎么办呢？

"我决定发明一种发明方法。"

在经过反复验证后，孙正义发现了三种发明模式。

第一种模式是问题解决法。实际需要是所有发明的源头，当一个人遇到问题时，就应该努力寻找解决这个问题的方法。

孙正义最喜欢的创意之一就是泡沫马桶座圈垫，这是他为了让人们在使用马桶座圈时，避免因为温度过高或过低产生不适感而发明的。吃比萨工具的发明同样采取了这种模式，解决了人们吃比萨时手上会沾油的问题。

第二种模式是横向思维法，即改变现有事物的成分、元素和属性。这是一种颠覆性的思考方式。改变事物的颜色、形状和大小，把黑的变成白的，方的变成圆的，大的变成小的，都是这种模式。

为视觉障碍者设计的交通信号灯的灵感便是来自这种思维模式。他已经做过假设，如果交通信号灯不是通过红色、绿色和黄色这些颜色来表示，而是用圆形、三角形和正方形这些形状来表示，会带来什么不同呢？

第三种模式是组合法，即将两种不同的东西结合在一起。举个简单的例子，把一块橡皮粘在铅笔上，或者把盒式磁带播放机和收音机结合起来发明一种新型的收录机。

孙正义的大多数创意都来源于第三种发明模式。

"这个方法有巨大的潜力，那是我在一年多的实践中得出的结论。"

因此，他特别为这种发明模式创建了一个结构化的系统。

首先，他准备了各种各样能组合的零部件：橙子、钉子、电脑内存卡……他把自己能想到的很多东西都写在了卡片上，最开始就有了大概300张这样的卡片。

其次，他给每个零部件都标上了不同的参数——成本、新奇的特性、对产品的了解程度，以及产品发明的可能性等。这些指标大约有40项，根据重要程度，他又把它们按照分值以5分、10分、30分等区分开来，这样一来，他就可以通过加减各项指标上的得分计算出总指标分值。

然后，他会随机选三个零部件，将它们结合起来。与此同时，他也会将这些零部件的总指标相乘，结果更好的组合就更有可能成为一项发明。

这样一来，所有零部件的组合方法就可以被大概估算出来，那就是 300×299×298÷3=8 910 200。

一开始他使用的是卡片，但由于组合数字太过庞大，之后他决定用计算机来完成这件事情。

他制作了一个表格，将这些零部件从高分到低分进行排列，把最高分的零部件用星号标记出来。他要做的事情就是将这些信息录入数据库，他只需要用键盘，就能提取出各种至关重要的信息。这样一来，孙正义就可以有保障地每天用5分钟时间想出一个发明。

他的"创意库"已经从笔记本转移到了计算机上，当他将其作为一个独立项目提交给学校时，主管教授给了他满分的评价。

这位教授说："你是我见过的第一位借助计算机完成发明创造的人。"

彼时，正如艾伦·凯所说，孙正义已经预见了计算机的未来。同时，他已经在为创造计算机的未来而努力。

计算机不会掠夺人类的创意，而会给人类的创造性思维插上翅膀，并让它翱翔。

截至目前，孙正义已拥有50多项发明专利——这些都是他创造未来所需的东西。

百万美元的合同

在加利福尼亚大学伯克利分校读书的第三年,孙正义创造了一个带有语音功能的电子翻译器。他的"创意库"大概记录了250多条创意,但这一次,他决定把精力集中在这一个创意上,并决心尽全力将它变成一款产品。孙正义的想法是将"字典""液晶显示屏""语音合成功能"这三个要素组合起来。

他设计了一个方案,在液晶显示屏上合成嵌入式键盘,这样,只要在键盘上打出一句话,系统就可以将这个文本翻译成9种不同的语言并且大声读出来。从本质上来说,这就是一种具有语音功能的电子翻译器。

在发明制作样品的过程中,孙正义的策略是多向这个领域的世界顶尖人才请教,听听他们的意见。

孙正义在数学、物理学和计算机科学等科目中取得了优异的成绩。

"我知道如果我下定决心去做,一定可以独立完成。"

然而,"单单开发出具有语音合成功能的产品就会花费我10年甚至20年的时间。人的一生只有区区几十年,创意虽然是我自己的,但是要想把它变为现实,就必须找一些相关领域的世界顶级专家来解决一些细节问题"。

孙正义翻开了他的电话簿，开始一通又一通地打电话。

这个领域的顶级专家都有谁呢？

他预约的第一个人是一位在语音合成方面的世界级权威，加利福尼亚大学伯克利分校空间科学实验室的物理学教授福雷斯特·莫泽。通过这位教授的推荐，他还联系到了查克·卡尔森，他可是参与设计过阿波罗宇宙飞船上使用的计算机硬件的"大牛"。

现在的问题变成了要怎样说服这些顶级专家与他合作，开展这项工作。

他饱含热情并满怀信心地向这些专家介绍了自己想做的事情："我将制造出世界上第一台具备语音合成功能的计算机。"

"我不知道自己是否会成功，但我坚信如果我们大家齐心协力，一定会取得成功。"他说，"最起码，我们奋斗在科技的最前沿，这项工作会为你们提供非常好的研究素材，这至少是一个探索的过程。"

孙正义得到的回复大概都是这样的："我明白，你的观点听起来也非常有趣，可是，你真的想清楚了要做这件事吗？"

面对这些专家的委婉拒绝，孙正义并没有放弃，他还为这些专家开出了一份薪酬清单。针对不同的人，他列出了不同的薪酬，例如，莫泽教授将在产品开发成功后收到一笔酬金；在查克之后负责硬件设计的亨利·赫特克斯将得到50美元/时的酬金；负责杂务工作的同学刘洪的年薪是2万美元，这与一名大学应届毕业生的工资相同。

明确的薪酬清单让这些人颇为震惊，他们很快意识到，孙正义是真的想要做成这件事情。

孙正义继续游说众人："这既是一次学习经验，也对世界有益，而且大家还可以收获不菲的薪酬。"

之后，这些顶级专家的态度也有了变化，他们开始陆续问孙正义："按照你的计划，我能做些什么呢？"

在这一过程中，我认为孙正义做到的最重要的事情就是保持自信，而且行事风格有说服力。

后来，我有机会请教了莫泽教授本人为什么会参与这个项目。教授说，当时关于电子翻译器的想法本身并没有给他留下什么特别的印象，"我喜欢的是他构思的销售策略，例如，将产品小型化并通过报刊亭销售"。

他们开始制造样品，虽然生产过程有一些延误，但最终还是圆满完成了。为此孙正义休学6个月，全身心地投入这个项目。

样品完成后，孙正义回到了日本，开始寻找买家。

他遇到的大多数公司都没有代理意向，也没有认真研究过他的产品。

但是，当他与当时日本最主要的电子产品制造厂夏普公司的经理面谈时，那位经理似乎对此产品有些兴趣。

面谈结束后，为了推动事情的进展，孙正义需要找到一位与夏普公司有过合作的专利律师。孙正义给许多人打了电话，最后，他登门拜访了一位专利律师，询问了关于自己的发明的价值问题，并了解到这项发明符合申请专利的条件。接着，孙正义打听到了夏普公司决策人的名字，消息得到确认后，他就请求这位律师打电话给这些人，并且告诉他们应该坐下来面对面地和他谈谈深度合作的事情。就是这样，孙正义通过努力，争取到了和时任夏普公司总经理佐佐木正面对面交流的机会。

结果是，他和夏普公司签订了一份价值1亿日元的经销许可合同。

孙正义更喜欢以美元为单位来说这个数字。

"百万美元的合同。"

"百万美元"带有一种光环，孙正义的心态始终保持得如同年轻时签订百万美元的合同一般。

孙正义开始发明是出于一份不能依赖父母生活补贴的责任感。这也成就了他与许多人的相遇，并将他带入了电子世界的内核。在这个世界里,他因计算机芯片的美丽而如此感动,以至流下了眼泪。在那里他迈出了很大的一步,并开始刻画一个光辉的未来。

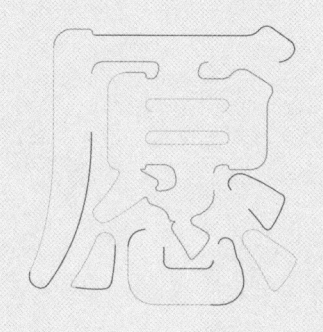

第三章
自我锤炼

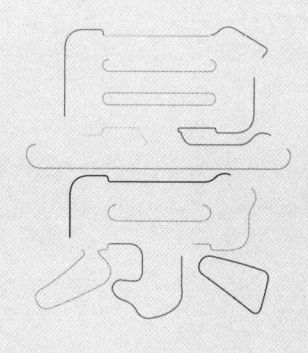

我只是不甘居于人后

1987年10月,我第一次采访孙正义,我对他当时说的话记忆犹新。

"我只是不甘居于人后。"

他语气激动,一遍又一遍地重复着。

"人生就像爬山,我想尽快登顶,如果做不到,我会感到非常沮丧。归根结底,我就是想要成为第一。"这种决心经常让他夜不能寐、辗转反侧。

孙先生身上的那种对争做第一近似疯狂的劲头和执着让人非常震惊。也许正是这种心态所带来的力量造就了他的性格。

孙先生接着谈了自己要成为企业家领头羊的原因。

"成为第一,才能熬过漫长的艰苦岁月。经济衰退时,先倒闭的往往是那些实力靠后的公司。"

1981年3月,也就是那次采访的6年前,孙先生在福冈市杂饷隈地区创立了一家市场调研公司。

这家公司的办公楼是一栋木结构的两层小楼,屋顶是铁皮做的,占地面积不到20平方米,差不多只有10个榻榻米那么大。小楼里面的房间没有空调,一打开办公室里的落地电风扇,纸片就会被吹得四处乱飞。

这家公司的成立并不以营利为目的,孙先生的雄心远高于此。通过这家公司,他想弄清楚最适合自己发展的领域,借此成就一番事业。他雇用了大量的员工做市场调研,为描绘属于自己的商业蓝图做准备。

显然,这家调研公司确实也没有盈利。

"什么产业能够在日本独领风骚呢?"

孙先生早就为此设定了一系列必要条件。

这个产业必须有广阔的发展前景,为了这个产业,孙正义愿意将他后半生的全部精力投入其中,而且,这个产业可能是集团未来发展战略的核心。同时,它一定是一个具有鲜明独特性的、其他人还未进入的领域,在未来10年,甚至更短的时间之内就能发展成为日本最强,并能在20世纪后半叶闻名全球。

因此，孙正义先生把调查范围缩小到了40个产业，他对这些产业都做了详尽的市场调研。调查的资料被一堆又一堆地收集了起来，每一堆都高达1米，要是把这些资料都堆在一起，则高达40多米。

孙先生研读了所有的资料，为每个产业拟定了暂时的商业计划，同时向日本各个产业内首屈一指的专家请教。只要找到这些专家的联系方式，他就会亲自打电话预约见面，孙先生的事务非常繁忙，所以他会邀请专家来福冈进行面谈，向这些专家请教自己的商业计划是否可行，并积极采纳那些具有建设性的意见。在这个过程中，孙先生不仅报销专家的所有费用，还会给他们丰厚的酬劳。

有一次，孙先生就站在用柑橘纸板箱搭建的临时舞台上给自己的员工发表了一场激情四射的演讲。

"5年内我们的销售额将突破100亿日元，10年内就将达到500亿日元。"

"最终，我们要实现的目标销售额是1万亿日元。"

听到他具有远大抱负的演讲，其中有两名员工从一开始便沉默不语，说到最后，他们甚至对孙正义"夸夸其谈"的演讲内容心生厌倦，最后干脆选择了离职。或许，他们认为这位孙先生太过疯狂，根本不值得与之共事。

1981年9月，也就是孙先生创办市场调研公司6个月之后，他创办了日本软银公司，最初它只是一家计算机套装软件经销公司，直到1982年，公司的经营范围开始涉及出版业务，专门出版与计算机相关的作品。

公司成立25年之后，也就是2005年，软银的财务报告显示其总销售额达到了1万亿日元，孙先生的"万亿梦"实现了。

"登上巅峰，成为第一之后，你所看到的风景将大为不同。"孙先生说。

他说，做生意就要勇夺第一，如果不争第一就不要做生意。

"因为如果不是第一，你就无法推出那些影响深远的变革策略。"

"在众多领域占据最大市场份额，并不断扩张，这的确是通往成功之路。"

"当你有信心在某个领域大展拳脚时，你就必须下定决心，争做第一。一旦下定决心，你就必须竭尽全力。"

孙先生的这种激情是他坚守的品质，至今分毫未减。

恩人感谢日

孙正义先生说："我现在的一切都起源于和我恩人的第一

次见面。"他口中的恩人就是夏普公司前副社长佐佐木正。

佐佐木正逝世于2018年1月31日，享年102岁，孙先生曾为此发表了情真意切的悼文。

"如果在公司创立之前我没有遇见佐佐木正先生，就不会有今天的我和软银集团。他是一个伟大的人，为日本高科技电子技术的发展奠定了基础。甚至可以说，他不仅是我和我公司的恩人，更是全体日本人民的恩人。"

在1977年，孙先生与佐佐木正第一次见面时，孙先生还是加利福尼亚大学伯克利分校的一名学生。

那时候，孙先生不愿意打零工，心里反倒想的是找一份一天只要花上5分钟、一个月就能挣100万日元的工作。所以他开始尝试各种发明创造，终于，他发明了一款带语音功能的电子翻译器。当时的夏普公司是日本的主流电子生产商之一，经过谈判，公司愿意花100万美元买下这款产品的专利权。时任夏普公司总经理的佐佐木正就是负责与孙先生商谈此事的人。

这件事情发生的时候，孙先生还没有创办软银公司，这也是他第一次赚到这么大一笔钱。

结束了与佐佐木正在大阪的商业谈判之后，孙先生回到学校又发现了一个商机：从日本购买街机游戏《太空侵略者》，并把它销往美国。之后他买下了一家游戏厅，制订了详尽的商业计划和日常财务核算计划，一个月后，这家游戏厅的营业额翻了3倍。

孙先生学生时期的成功创业经历为后来软银集团的创办奠定了基础，从始至终佐佐木正都支持孙先生。

佐佐木正是一名工程师，他因研制便携式计算机而出名，他很早便慧眼识珠，看出了孙先生的商业潜力。佐佐木正在中国台湾长大，毕业于京都大学，毕业后他一直在日本川西机械厂工作。二战时期，他接到军令被派去德国协助制造雷达设备，之后他被派去美国盟军最高司令部工作，在那里他学会了开发晶体管和改良真空电子管性能。战争结束后，他开始为夏普公司工作，佐佐木正提携帮助过很多商界的后起之秀，甚至连美国商业巨头史蒂夫·乔布斯都称其为良师。

孙正义先生和佐佐木正友谊深厚，他在加利福尼亚大学伯克利分校上学时，佐佐木正只要去美国出差便会与他共进晚餐，大约每两三个月一次。即使在孙先生创立了日本软银公司后，他们也经常相聚，不管孙先生的事业发展得多么好，佐佐木正总是会给出体贴入微、详细周到的意见。

孙先生为佐佐木正写的悼文中有这样一句话：

"即使在今天，佐佐木正先生的'共创哲学'仍是我们软银集团的核心。"

佐佐木正认为发明创造不是某一个天才人物独有创造力的产物，任何发明创造都得益于前人的研究成果。只有认同这个观念，我们才能进行良性竞争，而这才是孕育伟大发明的关键。孙先生完全接受并承袭了这种"共创精神"。

"佐佐木正先生这些年来对我毫不藏私，对此，我要表达自己衷心的感谢，并致以我最深切的悼念。

"第一次和他见面时，我既无丰富的商业经验，也无卓越的专业知识，有的只是满腔豪情壮志。"

其实，除了豪情壮志，孙先生还拥有激情和无与伦比的智慧，而正是这一点吸引了很多追随他的人。

在1981年公司创立之初和其后经历磨难，遇到风浪的时候，有许多人向孙先生伸出过援手。

为了铭记那时的感受，孙先生在5月的非国家节假日中选了一个工作日，并把这一天称为"恩人感谢日"。公司还把这一天定为公休日，在孙正义的眼里，这一天的重要性和公司的周年庆是一样的。

回顾公司的恩人及他们曾提供的帮助，所有人都可以感受到一种激情，正是这种激情帮助软银集团渡过了最开始的艰难时期。

软银集团的重要恩人包括但不限于下面这些人：

清水洋三。当年，经过一番调研之后，孙先生下定决心要创办一家在日本首屈一指的软件经销公司，于是他在1981年创办了日本软银公司。时任NAIGAI数据服务公司总经理的清水洋三是第一个对孙正义的事业成功深信不疑的人。他是孙先生的第一位供应商，为软银公司在大阪的电子产品展会供应了自己公司研发的软件。

川岛正英。清水洋三的朋友，时任《朝日新闻》周刊主编。在川岛正英的帮助下，孙先生结识了世界范围内很多在政治、商业、大众传媒及学术圈极具影响力的巨头。

田边聪。1981年，为了普及个人计算机，孙先生决定进军出版业，田边聪曾提出在全日本的书店出售"袖珍计算机图书馆"的想法，这便是袖珍计算机软件集。尽管孙先生并不了解出版业，但是在佐佐木正的帮助之下，孙先生见到了时任东京朝日屋书店总经理的田边聪。他请求田边先生帮忙联系出版社或者专营书店的经销商。出乎孙正义预料的是，当时田边聪爽快地答应了帮忙。因此，他也有恩于软银集团。

净弘博光。1981年，净弘博光时任上新电机株式会社社长，他在大阪成立了日本最大的个人计算机商店——J&P（现上新电机）。他当时就做出了一个惊人的决定——把软银集团列为软件独家供应商，这为软银市场影响力的提升添彩不少。

藤原睦朗。他是净弘博光公司的高级职员，时任上新电机株式会社销售经理。

工藤裕司和工藤浩。当时他们两兄弟分别担任日本游戏公司哈德森公司的董事长和总经理，该公司开发了许多热门游戏。在收了3 000万日元押金后，他们同意将公司的游戏版权独家提供给软银集团。

御器谷正之。他是第一劝业银行麹町分行的经理。1982年软银集团支付给哈德森公司3 000万日元押金之后，公司运营资金所剩无几，正是御器谷正之竭尽全力帮助软银最终通过免抵押担保贷款的方式筹得资金，佐佐木正也为促成此事耗了颇多精力，费了不少唇舌。

大内淳义。他是日本电气股份有限公司的副总裁，日本电气股份有限公司是日本主流电子公司之一。1982年，孙先生决定在电视上宣传自己公司的计算机杂志，这在当时算是个新鲜事物。大内淳义当即决定出资3 000万日元，占公司广告支出的一半之多。

孙先生对待生活积极乐观的态度吸引了这些人。

"生活是如此美妙！一分一秒我都不想浪费。同时我对万事万物充满了感激之情。"孙先生笑着说道。这种坚持让人钦佩，孙先生也一直在回报那些曾帮助过他的人。

"我不会背叛那些信任我的人。"

他在生活中结识了许多人，克服并迎接了许多困难和挑战。

"于我而言，世界上最开心的事情就是不断寻求新的挑战，只要一直追求新事物，你的生活就会变得意义非凡。这简直美妙至极。"

成功不能仅靠聪明

野田一夫是一名商业领域的学者，因担任彼得·德鲁克《管理的实践》一书的日文版总编辑一职而出名，《管理的实践》日文版是自由国民社于1956年出版发行的。1981年，年仅24岁的孙先生第一次去位于东京赤坂的办公室拜访野田一夫时，软银公司刚刚成立不久。

孙先生给野田一夫留下了深刻的印象。

"他个子不高，是个非常出色的年轻人，脸上总是挂着诚恳的笑容。"

那时候，野田一夫的办公室学术氛围浓厚，经常有年轻的企业家来访，就管理学问题进行辩论，其中两位后来和孙先生一起被誉为"初创企业三剑客"。他们是 HIS 国际旅行社[①]现任董事长兼总裁泽田秀雄和保圣那集团[②]负责人南部靖之。

有一次，野田问他们："你们觉得什么是志向，什么是梦想呢？"

"梦想是欲望，如房子、车，而志向是未来要迎接的挑战。执着欲望不可取，成就远大志向才是正道！"野田说。

孙先生深以为然，他把这句话深深地记在了心里。

"孙正义为人处世说不上风度翩翩，但作为一个不容忽视的大人物，却也没有丝毫盛气凌人。在取得了这么多成就后，他依然能保持谦卑的态度，实属不易。"野田先生是这么评价孙正义的。

孙先生给大多数人留下了友好、谦逊的印象。

野田认为，孙先生能在残酷的商业界大获成功，谦逊就是秘诀。

作为一名商业学者，野田先生见过很多怀揣着企业家梦想的年轻人，也正是这个原因，野田先生有一种慧眼识人的能力。

[①] HIS 国际旅行社：1980 年由泽田秀雄创办，截至 2018 年 10 月，总销售额为 7 285 亿日元。

[②] 保圣那集团：1976 年由南部靖之创办，截至 2019 年 5 月，总销售额为 3 269 亿日元。

野田曾说："如果用一个词来概括孙正义，那就如他的名字一般——正义。"

草率、肤浅这些词汇与孙先生完全挨不上边儿，埋头奋进才是他的全部。

1982年，日本软银公司成立不久，桥本五郎便加入了公司，经过多年的努力奋斗，他最终坐上了软银集团出版部门负责人的位置。桥本五郎生前回忆起孙先生对他说过的话时，认为令他印象最深刻的是这句话：

"五郎（桥本的名字），如果可以选择做一个聪明人，或者一个愚直诚实但凡事坚持到底的人，你会选哪一种？如果让我来选，答案毫无疑问是后者。"

受孙先生的启发，桥本五郎在工作上越发诚恳，越发坚持到底。

当然，多年来也有出于各种原因选择离开软银集团的人。但是，他们中很多人回忆起在软银集团工作的时光时，总是不加掩饰地流露出浓浓的柔情。"在软银工作很辛苦，被孙先生骂也是家常便饭。但是，只要你足够真诚，孙先生还是会给予谅解的。"

孙先生会时不时重复："一个人光聪明是远远不够的，只有不自欺欺人、深入学习，才能真正成长。"

2019年8月，一位年轻的企业主收到了孙先生的邮件，开头是这样写的："鄙人才疏学浅，请多关照。"要知道，只有年轻职员写信才常常以这样的措辞开头，孙先生的谦逊低调通过这封信件的开头可见一斑。

但是，这番话却是孙先生的肺腑之言。

只要有七成胜算，那就全力冲刺

孙先生20多岁时就形成了基本的哲学观——"孙孙兵法"[①]，这种哲学思想受到了中国古代军事理论作品，伟大的军事家孙武所著的《孙子兵法》的影响和启发，孙正义先生在横竖各5格的棋盘状网格的每个格子中都写了一个字（见图1）。这个25字策略不仅代表了孙先生的人生哲学，也根植于他的商业哲学。

其中最能体现孙先生独创性的是"顶情略七斗"，这是一种日语词序的表达，很好地展现了孙先生的眼界。

---

① 孙正义酷爱《孙子兵法》，病中也坚持研读，心得颇丰。他独创了一套"孙孙兵法"，这种创新性应用明显地表现在他的企业经营管理中，"孙孙兵法"名字的由来是因为他自己也姓孙，将"孙子"的"孙"与"孙正义"的"孙"组合起来，同时，他也自称是孙武的子孙。——译者注

道	天	地	将	法
顶	情	略	七	斗
一	流	攻	守	群
智	信	仁	勇	严
风	林	火	山	海

注释：孙正义借鉴中国古代著名军事家孙武的《孙子兵法》制定出了自己的25字经营方针。灰色部分是孙正义原创，其余为孙武的原字。

孙先生将这25个字视为应在经商活动和商业决策中考虑的因素。

第1行的"道天地将法"表示在战斗中取胜的条件，"道"即理念。

第2行的"顶情略七斗"表示领导者应该拥有的智慧，"顶"即最高点。

第3行的"一流攻守群"表示力争第一的经营方式，"一流"即全心投入，力争第一。

第4行的"智信仁勇严"表示领导者必备的才能与领悟能力。

第5行的"风林火山海"表示商战的方法。

图1 "孙孙兵法"图

"顶"是最高点的意思，在孙先生的思想体系中指目标、目的地，或者说是眼界。

"只要一个人下定了决心，明确了自己的人生目标就是攀登山峰，那么他的人生规划和成就也就明确了一半。因此，拥有什么样的眼界，对一个人的人生来说极其重要。"

明确自己未来的路径，定下目标完成的期限，10年还是30年？期限必须十分明确。不仅如此，我们还要具体、生动地事先设定自己取得成功后的愿景。

"情"是数据信息，特别指商场数据信息的收集与分析。

"收集数据信息，描绘未来愿景。愿景一旦设定，接下来就是非常谨慎细致、全面彻底地获取各种数据信息的过程。通过这个过程，我们还可以检验预设的愿景是否准确恰当。"

不论是开创新业务还是投资新项目，孙先生在每次做出商业决定并付诸行动之前，都会对获得的信息进行充分分析。

"略"是策略。

策略是在权衡利弊，绞尽脑汁综合考虑所有相关因素之后所得出的结论。在这个过程中，我们要考虑的应该是，也只能是对事情发展起到决定性作用的因素。

接着是数字"七"。

孙先生说："在我的整体策略中，7是一个很关键的数字。"

"如果事情发展到了已然有九成或90%的胜算才采取行动，结果就会不尽如人意。一般来说，等到事情已经有90%的胜算时，就代表已经错过了很多时机，这时候再采取行动可能为时已晚。因为这个时候竞争对手也在伺机而动,为了不落后于人,我们必须先发制人。"

虽说如此,但也不是说越早采取行动就越好。

"在事情发展还只有五成或六成胜算时就决然行动,可能会让自己陷入极大的危险之中,要么取得全面胜利,大杀四方,要么输得干干净净,倾家荡产。"

由此,孙先生就总结出了自己的经商攻略。

"这就是为什么我会说,有七成胜算时就是最佳的冲刺时机。"

我们看到"七"时还要联想到"三",这个"三"代表了退却的勇气。

孙先生说道:"之所以说七成胜算最好,是因为这是我经过深思熟虑后才得出的结论,我对此深信不疑。"

从另外一个角度考虑,孙先生的策略也反映了一个问题。如果一件事情失败的概率大于三成,那么,我们就应该考虑是否要去做这件事。而当失败的概率不到三成时,哪怕你是冒险而为最后失败了,纵然不能全身而退,也会因为及时撤出而不至于满盘皆输。"自然界中也有这样的现象,一只蜥蜴如果只断掉三成的尾巴,就可以再长回来,但如果半条尾巴都断掉了,蜥蜴就会因器官衰竭而死亡。"孙先生这样补充解释了他的思想。

孙先生还说,勇往直前固然重要,但能及时止损更为不易。

你可以这样想一想,如果一辆汽车没有刹车或是无法倒车,该有多么可怕!

"固执己见、盲目向前的人是当不好领军人物的!"

孙先生还说:"一旦发现败局已定,只要时机成熟,跑!跑得越快越好!不要害怕有失体面,也不要顾及他人的看法。及时撤出阵地!不能意气用事地继续苦战下去。"

其实,直面挑战、热爱挑战使孙先生在商界获得了极大的赞誉,孙先生并不畏惧挑战,他不仅偏爱冒险,甚至在很多商业决策中都掺杂了赌的成分。事实上,代表了孙先生商业眼界的"顶情略七斗"中的"斗"就是指斗争精神。崇高的理想、丰富的数据信息、周密的策略,即使是这些再加上七成胜算也并不能保障成功,拼搏奋斗才是取胜的不二法宝。因此,孙先生才会时常几乎倾尽所有,为了美好的愿景而奋斗。

虽然如此,孙先生的行事风格却是极其谨慎的。

孙先生的弟弟孙泰藏也是一名企业家、投资家,他用了一个非常贴切而有趣的比喻来说明哥哥孙正义的行事原理。"我哥是个极为谨慎的人。'过石桥之前还要敲一敲。'这是在日本流传很广的一句俗语,用来描述那些做事过度谨慎小心的人,而我哥就是这样的人，他过石桥前不仅要敲，还要反复地敲，他甚至会避开某些石桥。但一旦确定了那座石桥可以通过，他就会开着卡车轰然而过，毫不犹豫。"

孙正义先生本人也说过很多类似的话：

"固执己见的人是傻瓜。"

"不愿后退的人是笨蛋。"

"不肯撤离的人是执拗鬼。"

"我并没有给自己的经商范围设定限制，我可能涉足任何行业，但前提是，如果我从某个领域退出来，我的核心产业也必须做到稳如泰山。这样，我可以不断尝试新事物，也可以毫无顾虑地撤出。"

"这样做可能会让人觉得我不会从挫折中吸取教训，但事实并非如此。"

孙先生在说这些话时，表情严肃认真。

其实，孙先生的经历告诉我们，一位商人的成功秘诀，可以用八个字概括：无畏退却，成就大业。

冥思苦想

在软银集团成立之初，井上雅博和宫内谦就与孙先生相识了。

井上雅博于1987年进入软银综合研究所，1992年加入软银公司，与孙先生同岁的他头脑冷静、很有主见。1994—1996年，井上担任首席执行官办公室执行秘书一职。

"孙总裁行事专注力极强，令人惊讶。有一次，他因为完全沉浸在思考之中，走路的时候竟然撞上了电线杆。"

孙先生于1996年1月成立雅虎日本（现雅虎日本控股公司）。公司成立后，井上就是孙先生最倚重的顾问。同年7月，井上获得提拔，升为公司总裁，一路引领雅虎日本走向了今日的辉煌。2012年，井上从雅虎日本辞职。2017年他因车祸不幸逝世。以下是他生前对孙先生的评价：

"一方面，他充满活力，具有大局意识；另一方面，他对数字和其他细节无比专注。这是我最佩服他的地方，很多人可能具备其中的某一方面，但两方面兼具的人少之又少。"

宫内谦是现任软银集团总裁。他于1984年加入软银公司，之后一直坚守在公司的管理一线。作为孙先生的得力干将，他被孙先生亲切地称为内谦。2003年，他曾经这样评价他的上司孙正义：

"孙总裁的优点就是善于用人，他开会不仅仅是给大家分享信息。例如，在收购公司和进行谈判时，大家会讨论谁是参与此事的最佳人选。这个时候，孙先生往往会打破砂锅问到底，层层分析，直到大家讨论出这个最佳人选。在这个过程中，通常既掺杂着理性因素又混合着情感因素，而孙先生能够非常好地将二者平衡，做出最有利于公司的决策。"

孙先生也曾说过，软银集团的会议是开放式的，不像某些公司的会议气氛常常令人紧张不安。

"我认为公司会议不是个人的脱口秀场，事实上，在我们公司的会议讨论过程中经常出现争议，总裁的提议也时常被否决。"

在软银集团的会议上，不管职位高低，任何人都可以畅所欲言。自公司成立以来，这种氛围就一直保持着。

孙正义说过："我们绞尽脑汁，极其细致地思考每一个问题，确保问题的方方面面都被考虑到。我们不断设想问题发展到最糟糕时的经济状况，然后逐一思考解决办法，直至得到最便于操作并且行之有效的解决方案。"

"右脑负责生想法，左脑负责分析落实想法的细节。只有左右脑同时考虑问题，形成的想法才具有说服力和可行性。"

"用数据思考问题，用理性解决问题。"

"一个人头脑聪明固然很重要，但归根结底，拥有持之以恒的行事品质才能取得成功。不服输、不放弃、始终保持热情是一个人取得成功的必备特征。"

"实现梦想的要点就是对梦想保持长久的热情。"

孙先生、井上和宫内有共同的观念。"哪怕当眼前看起来已经没有更好的方式来解决一件事情时,我们还是不能放弃,而是要沉下心来,再想想看。"

孙先生往往会尽可能听取更多人的意见,经过深思熟虑之后,再做决定。

宫内直接而准确地总结道:"孙先生怀有崇高的使命感。"

正是这一点成就了今天的孙正义。

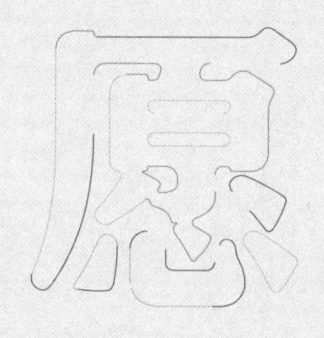

第四章
战略与筹划

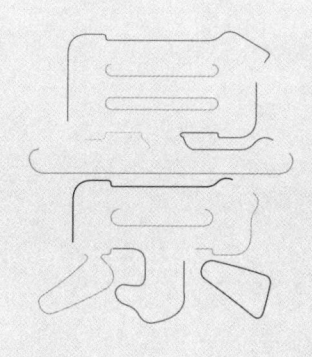

企业管理的核心是管控黄色区域

"你根本就没有完整的战略,你懂什么是战略吗?"孙正义有些严厉地训斥着自己的弟弟孙泰藏。

孙泰藏已经参加了两次东京大学的入学考试,但都以名落孙山告终,当时,他正在为第三次报考东京大学做准备。那是1992年,为了考试,孙泰藏甚至决定独自一人住在东京备考。就在这种情况下,哥哥孙正义决定找他面对面地谈一谈这件事情。

孙正义比弟弟泰藏年长15岁,九州地区向来重视对长者要绝对服从这一传统。而作为哥哥,孙正义是长辈,拥有绝对的权威。

泰藏咕哝道："反正我就是比别人差，也不是非得上东京大学，或许我根本没有上大学的必要。"

孙正义听了勃然大怒："这就不是你想不想上大学或者想上哪所大学的问题！"

孙正义想知道，他的弟弟到底是否"拼尽了全力"。

"你呆坐在这里愤世嫉俗，为自己找借口，对自己、对社会、对一切都装作漠不关心，敷衍了事，过着行尸走肉般的生活，你开心吗？"

"不，我讨厌这样的人生。"

"这就关乎你的人生态度问题。"

这场谈话持续了一个多小时，对泰藏而言，哥哥的言语无异于在他的伤口上撒盐，深深地刺激了他。

"不要使失败成为惯性，不要让自己成为失败者！"

随后，孙正义详细而认真地向弟弟讲述了他人生战略的谋划之道。

"你一定觉得你每天都在努力做自己力所能及的事情吧？"孙正义告诫他，"但这是不够的。"

"战略的本质，在于你如何分配你所掌握的资源。

"最终的结果究竟如何，没有人能保证。但有些事是完全可以做到的：精确地计算出要通过这场考试你所要付出的努力的总数值。要看多少教科书和参考书,做多少练习题才能通过考试,这些都是可以量化的。"

孙正义要求孙泰藏必须将自己要面对的这些任务非常具体地推算并列举出来。但是弟弟觉得这对他来说太难了,孙正义也为此降低了要求和标准。

他说,如果很难做到把所有事情量化,那就去把你能找到的所有学习资料都买回来。

"去八重洲图书中心,把全部相关学习资料都买回来。"孙正义这样要求刚搬到东京的孙泰藏。东京有一家名为八重洲图书中心的大型书店,那里的参考书的齐全程度远远超出了他的想象。

泰藏打电话向父亲求助:"我要买参考书,请您借给我10万日元,日后我一定连本带利还给您。"

他买了许多用来装参考书的纸箱,每看完一本参考书,就花30分钟的时间完成相应的练习题。他估算了自己在30分钟内能写多少页练习题,以及读完一本书要花多长时间。在此基础上,他以小时为单位,制订了年度学习计划表,每天设定16个小时的学习时间。也就是说,在考试前他还有5 760个小时可以学习。

他从哥哥那里学到了一个"商业计划制订秘籍",即为自已建立一个缓冲区，用以应对预期与实际相背离的突发情况。上午8点至中午为第一阶段，在这段时间里，每隔一小时换一本参考书学习。具体要读哪本书，读哪几页，都被详细列在了年度计划表里。

从中午到下午1点为缓冲时间，这段时间在计划表上是空白的。在这段时间里，可以将上午没能按计划完成的部分补回来。

下午1点至5点为第二阶段。而下午5点至6点则是另一个缓冲时间。

即便如此，依旧会出现超出计划的情况，因此，孙泰藏又留出了周日上午作为缓冲时间。周日上午，他会将本周所有未能完成的事情做完。倘若还是没能按计划完成，就预留出每个月月底的最后一天来完成原定计划。

他把制订计划的过程比作修建水坝，即使有些水坝的接缝处不是很严实，有些东西会从中漏出来，他也会想办法把它们逐步放回去。因为他每天要修建的"水坝"可不止一座，遗漏的部分就在每个周末修补完毕，如果还是不行，月底之前他也会将漏洞完全封住。

如果事情进展得顺利，按计划完成，他会在计划表中把这部分涂成绿色；如果计划因为一些不可控的外在因素或自身的惰性而没能完成，就涂成红色；如果只完成了一半，则涂成黄色。

一个月后，孙正义询问孙泰藏学习计划的进展情况——这就像是在检查孙泰藏的年中商业计划报告。

孙泰藏的年度计划表上还有不少没有完成的部分涂着红色，他本以为哥哥会责备他，但出乎意料的是，孙正义并没有这样做。

"黄色部分代表的是什么？"

孙正义根本没有关注表格中的红色部分，但说话时的表情却很严肃。

"翻到标为黄色所代表的部分，告诉我你对这部分内容的完成情况是怎么样的？"

"做了一半。"孙泰藏回答道。

"现在我给你出一张试卷。"孙正义当场出了一些英语考试题目，而孙泰藏的正确率只有20%~30%。

"你说你做了一半，那这个测试结果又意味着什么呢？"

"嗯……我不明白为什么会这样。"

"你这是在自欺欺人，这是一份虚假的工作报告。报告中显示你完成了一半，但实际上你并没有完成一半。"孙正义再一次告诫弟弟，"人性往往是软弱的，因为无论是谁都想让别人看到自己好的一面，所以分明只做了1/3，却偏偏要说做了一半。"

"你报告中没有完成的红色部分其实无可厚非，我暂且不提。因为红色意味着事情没有任何进展，也没有丝毫回旋的余地。但黄色部分就要进行认真分析了……"

当时，孙正义创办的软银公司发展平顺，正在步入正轨。他拿自己公司的情况作为例子讲给弟弟听。

"软银公司现在有3 000名员工，如果所有员工在报告工作进度时都谎称他们完成了一半的工作量，而实际上只做了1/3，那么我们的预期和实际绩效之间就会出现巨大的偏差。要知道，企业经营管理的本质就在于如何管控好这些黄色区域。"

哥哥的教诲使孙泰藏从此拥有了更加坚定的信念。功夫不负有心人，孙泰藏在东京大学的模拟考试中排名全国第二，最终获得了东京大学的入学资格。在校期间，他还创办了自己的公司，在经营和管理公司方面，他一直将哥哥孙正义的教导记在心里，这对他产生了极其深远的影响。

人生就像玩《超级玛丽》游戏

2000年，互联网泡沫破灭了。

那一年孙泰藏 28 岁，是一家网站设计和系统开发公司的董事长，管理着大约 80 名员工。突如其来的经济风暴彻底改变了他的生活，所有预先安排好的工作都被取消了，一时间公司四面楚歌，他实在不知道该如何应对这一危机。他怎样做才能给这么多员工按时发放工资呢？在经营公司方面，他的资历尚浅，不知道该如何处理与银行相关的事情，也没有大量的人脉资源。

"当时，我觉得自己走投无路了。"他被逼入了绝境，几近崩溃。

就在这个时候，他的哥哥孙正义约他一起吃饭。

哥哥像往常一样，激情澎湃地跟他谈论着互联网的光明前景。然而，弟弟却情绪低落、如鲠在喉，跟哥哥借钱的话怎么也说不出口。当他们起身准备离开，孙泰藏终于鼓起勇气想说出那句话时，却被哥哥抢了先。

"你要钱的话，我是不会借给你的。"

"我这不是没有办法了吗！"孙泰藏对哥哥的直白感到非常诧异。

"你的想法都写在你的脸上了，我是不会借给你一分钱的。"

听了哥哥的话，孙泰藏不禁苦笑。

与父亲一样，哥哥孙正义也很善于洞察人心，说话总是一针见血,直接将球抛回给对方。

"你需要多少钱?"孙正义问道。

弟弟没有绕弯子,直接回答说:"1 500万日元,我真的试过所有的方法了。"

孙正义说:"1 500万日元对你来说算是一笔巨款吧?而我也正在为如何筹集150亿日元而苦恼。"

然后他直截了当地说:"你需要1 500万日元,我不是不能借给你,但这对你来说没有任何好处。"

孙正义以玩电子游戏的攻略方法打比方,给弟弟解释了他不借钱的缘由。

"你还没通过《超级玛丽》的第1关,马上就会被最低级、武力最弱的敌人疾风龟击败,你甚至连第一朵云都跳不上去。"他说,"我已经通过了15~20层关卡,这是相当困难的。对我来说,教你如何通过走捷径到达第3关是很容易的,但是,如果你是依靠我直接告诉你的方法通过这一关的话,就算你最后到了第3关,也会被那一关的疾风龟秒杀掉。要知道,走捷径过关的办法,对你的未来是毫无意义的。"

接着,孙正义说出了他克服困难的核心方法。

"行事不疯狂,你就无法跨过坎坷。放手去撞南墙吧,只要你试遍了所有可能解决问题的办法,即便会撞得粉身碎骨,即便会变得一无所有，又能怎样呢？

"换言之，完全靠机会和运气误打误撞地找出路是行不通的。在第1关时，你必须让自己置身于陷阱与敌人之中，让自己为其所困，只有当你对这一关的情形了如指掌时，才能进入第2关。然后将第2关的敌人全部消灭后再进入第3关。这样即便你在通过某一关时死掉了，在重新开始时你还可以很快就赶上之前的水平。但是如果你单纯凭借运气或机会，就算侥幸闯到第8关，一旦你被杀死，再从第1关重新来过，你还是会感到非常困难。"

这番话不无道理，孙正义这个比喻很有说服力。

孙正义最后对他的弟弟说："我可以借钱给你，但是不是要用借来的钱渡过难关，你自己做决定。"

"不！不！"孙泰藏连忙拒绝，"听完你的这番话，我怎么可能还会向你借钱呢？"

他发现自己竟然笑了起来，感觉豁然开朗了。一开始，哥哥孙正义直白的说辞确实让他很气愤，然而，现在他却出奇的平静，仿佛心里的一块大石头落了地。

"生活就像玩《超级玛丽》游戏！"

生活不就和游戏闯关一样吗？孙泰藏想，既然如此，他决定用自己的智慧和策略来通关。

"但凡没有使你灭亡的挫折,终将使你更加强大。"

和哥哥一起吃完晚饭后,孙泰藏就去一个接一个地拜访了自己的客户,寻求解决问题的办法。

他还有很多工作要做,例如,虽然网站设计的预算被大幅削减了,但是工作还是照样要完成。在与客户的沟通过程中,孙泰藏坦诚地说出了项目的真实成本,他还直接表明了自己愿意以成本价承接项目。这意味着他们的成交价格将减半,甚至连半价都不到。除了价格,他还承诺自己会缩短工期,提前完成这些项目。

"真的吗?"客户大多露出了难以置信的表情。

"是的。"孙泰藏信心满满地说,"但是我这么做是有条件的……我需要您先支付一半的定金,这个建议您能接受吗?"

孙泰藏想清楚了,无论削减多少利润都不重要,只要他们有足够的现金流去周转,公司就不会破产。

接下来的洽谈都很顺利,客户接二连三地接受了他的条件,和他签下了一笔又一笔订单。

后来,当孙泰藏回想起那段日子时,常常感慨万分地说:"我去拜访那些客户的时候坦诚地表达了自己的想法。我想,当时他们一定感受到了我的决心。"

在哥哥孙正义"严苛的爱"的鞭策下,孙泰藏靠自己的力量通过了《超级玛丽》的第 1 关，渡过了那段非常困难的时期。

此后，孙泰藏成了一名后劲十足的创业者，最终创立了美思乐通公司，致力于解决世界重大课题，促进人才培养和创业投资，为社会发展创造有利条件。

他曾向一些乌克兰企业家讲起自己这个关于"超级玛丽"的故事，这些企业家非常认同故事中的观点。孙泰藏常常将爱沙尼亚和乌克兰称为"最令人兴奋的国家"。在这两个国家，初创企业数量的增长速度快到令人不可思议。

我之所以出离愤怒，是因为我对成功的渴望无人能及

"我之所以出离愤怒，是因为我对成功的渴望无人能及。"

2001 年 1 月 6 日，日本颁布了《建立先进信息与电信网络协会基本条例》（即《IT 基本法》）。依据该法律，政府将推动各种与互联网相关的基础设施的建设和规章制度的完善。

"时机到了。我一直在等待这一天。"

这是互联网泡沫破灭后的第二年，软银集团的股价跌到了谷底。

"我们没有钱，可是如果现在还不进军互联网领域，我们

什么时候才能在这个领域占有一席之地呢？"

这是一场孤注一掷的挑战。

"我得倾尽所有，冒险一搏。"

孙正义决定把公司的所有资源都投入宽带建设。

当时日本互联网的主流联网方式是拨号上网，与已经在网络建设各方面领先很多的韩国相比有很大的差距。韩国已经大力推动了宽带数字用户线路建设，用户可以独享带宽并能够长时间在线。

孙正义计划将被揶揄为"世界上网速最慢，但收费最高"的日本互联网打造成为"世界上网速最快，收费最低"的互联网体系。他已为即将到来的战斗做好了准备。此外，他秉持一个独特的理念，那就是一定要提供世界一流的宽带式互联网体系。

2001年6月19日，软银科技公司宣布成立雅虎日本，这项服务提供的宽带速度约为当时互联网巨头日本电报电话公司的4倍，价格却只相当于其1/4。消息一出，一夜之间就有18万人预约申请了这项宽带服务。

但是，宽带线路却无法在短期内完成铺设联通。于是，顾客的投诉接连不断，如不间断轰炸一般，其中一部分客户甚至需要等待6个月才能完成宽带安装。

在日本，要想开办宽带业务，就必须租借日本电报电话公司各个区域中心机房里的网络设备，但其光纤铺设工程却被严重推迟，效率低下。显然，这是对手日本电报电话公司的有意为之。

虽然孙正义多次要求日本电报电话公司解决问题，但情况并没有得到好转。孙正义终于忍不住，勃然大怒。同年6月29日，孙正义面色铁青，大步流星地走进日本网络监管局。

他疾言厉色地吼道："事情不能一直这么拖下去。如果你们监管部门还是无法与日本电报电话公司做好协调工作，所有问题还是得不到解决，我就在这里让你们难堪！"

说这些话时，他的态度极其认真。

"我会在新闻发布会上向用户致歉，告知他们我们不得不中断雅虎日本业务的原因，向他们解释为什么我们无法及时为他们提供宽带服务。但致歉之后，我会回到现在我站着的这个地方。"

经过这么一闹，没过多久，宽带安装的相关工作就开始有序地推进了。

两年后，即2003年，国际电信联盟认定，日本宽带在"高速与价廉"方面的综合得分位居世界第一。孙正义实现了他"让日本网速成为第一"的目标。

"信息革命带给所有人快乐。"孙正义是这么说的，也是这么做的。

与坂本龙马一起为建设新日本而献出生命的西乡隆盛说过："不惜命、不求名、不谋官、不贪财者，是无敌的。"① 孙正义就是这样一种怀有武士精神的人。

"我希望，在未来的某一刻，人们能因为我所创造的东西而感到愉悦、幸福。"

他竭力实现这个商业目标，为的不是一己私欲，而是希望日本的网络用户能因此获益。

正是孙正义的"愤怒"掀起了日本的这场互联网革命。

愤怒，有时具有无法估量的革新力量。

若员工考虑一步，则企业家应该考虑三百步

"企业家应该为企业发展殚精竭虑。"

---

① 西乡隆盛（1828—1877年）：日本江户时代末期生于萨摩藩，以下级武士的身份起家，参与发动了"王政复古"政变，助推了江户幕府向明治政府的政权过渡，最后兵败死于西南战争。司马辽太郎的小说《恰似飞翔》中就描写过他追求纯粹、学不成名死不还的信条，而这使他在日本备受企业经营者的追捧。《西乡南洲翁遗训》中就收录了这句话。

孙正义继续和弟弟聊着经商的事情,他问弟弟:"假设把员工为公司所做的事理解为 1 步,在这种情况下,企业家应该为公司做多少呢?"

孙正义和孙泰藏两兄弟在家里经常这样讨论商业问题,而讨论的话题往往就是他们日常在企业管理过程中所遇到的问题。孙泰藏思考后说出了自己的看法:"企业家应事无巨细地考虑到企业运营中的所有细节,这一点是毫无疑问的,比员工所考虑的应该多上三五倍,但是我认为孙正义之所以是孙正义,那所思所做肯定远高于此。"

所以他说:"或许是 10 倍?"

孙正义非常生气:"愚蠢!企业家的所思所想必须是员工的 300 倍还要多。"

听到这话,孙泰藏感到非常震惊。

这就是孙泰藏从哥哥孙正义那学来的,企业家应具备什么样的思维方式。

另一个例子是当你不得不说服一个人时,你该怎么做。

人们至少有上百条理由拒绝你的提议。你要想想有什么方法能让他们信服于你。你应该备足一套答案,以便完美应答所有对你的提议进行反驳的言论。

孙正义说:"切记不要强词夺理或是强行说服他们,如果你不能给予一个符合他们逻辑的答案,一切都只是徒劳。"

从那时起,孙泰藏每次谈判前都会预先罗列一些对方可能会用来拒绝提案的理由,并准备好对应的回答。当他将这些付诸实践后,方才意识到自己过去的观点有多么片面。

"这真的是一门大学问,从逻辑上理解和真正理解后付诸实践之间存在很大的差异。"

孙正义经常被称作"杀智王",这是一个日本俚语,指非常擅长赢得比他年长的男性支持的人。

甚至在软银集团的缔造过程中,许多商界大人物就好像被他的某种魅力吸引了一样,愿意帮助他取得最终的成功,缔造一个传奇。尽管只是一种可能性,但他们愿意在孙正义身上下注"豪赌"。

也许是孙正义的气质影响了周围的人,使他赢得了他们的支持。但归根到底,他的高度说服力来自他做事前那种近似疯狂的劲头和他所做的那些周全到令人难以置信的准备工作。

"如果员工想到的是1步,那么企业家必须想到300步,还要从反面考虑几十种,甚至上百种可能出现的情况来佐证之前的想法。"孙正义给他的弟弟孙泰藏的许多经验教训都有一个鲜明的特征,那就是工作量极大。例如,他应该反复核对

1 000 个甚至 10 000 个管理指数，被称为"1 000 探索法"和"10 000 探索法"，即尽一切可能探索所有情况 1 000 次或 10 000 次，以此获得数据信息并对它们进行分析。

孙正义曾对孙泰藏说自己的商业思维模式和漫画《巨人之星》①中的"棒球特训法"非常相似。在昭和时代，日本的经济快速恢复并高速增长，社会上普遍推崇斯巴达式的严苛训练法。孙正义在少年时期就受到《巨人之星》漫画的影响，为了增强腿部力量从而踢好足球，他甚至尝试穿着铁鞋坚持训练。

作为一名企业家，孙正义在提到这种斯巴达式艰苦训练的象征意义时，想要表达的是什么呢？

也就是说，成功不仅仅是"做什么"，更重要的是"做多少"。孙正义所获得的卓越成就未必就是他的商业战略运作成功的结果，而是在完成战略决策之后所做的事：在战术上的落实，在实践中的贯彻。

此时看来，如果存在所谓成功的诀窍，其背后都蕴藏着

---

① 《巨人之星》：一部 20 世纪六七十年代在日本男孩中非常受欢迎的棒球漫画。其主人公星飞雄马在父亲的指导下接受了非常严格的高强度训练，立志要成为父亲曾经效力的著名职业棒球队中的顶级投手，"巨人队的明星"。

非常简单的因果关系，"一分耕耘，一分收获"。在所有的商业领域和行业中，成功和失败的区别在于你准备得多么充分彻底、你的战略决策有多么有效完善、你的毅力恒心有多么强大。

孙泰藏感慨道："其实保持恒心是最难的，一个人总是重复一成不变的工作，而且一时又看不到显著的结果，即便是在整件事情刚刚开始时，也有可能因为坚持不下去而放弃。也许正是因为如此，成功的案例才寥寥无几。"

他哥哥给予他的教导是一以贯之的，不论他的表述如何变化，他总是在一次次强调着同一点。因此，孙泰藏说："我认为这是成功的最大秘诀。"

做好多手准备

"如果你已经着手做一件事了，那么你觉得应该为无法预见的情况做多少准备呢？"

就如往常一样，孙正义会冷不丁地抛给孙泰藏一个问题，虽然说话语气像是闲谈，但内容常常让他猝不及防，因为孙泰藏以前还真没有想过这些问题。

"嗯……我想说的是……为了应对事情发展不顺利或者不

在预料之中的情况，我会事先做好预备方案……你的意思是连这个替代方案也行不通时，还要有其他备选方案吗？"

孙正义对孙泰藏说："对，你一般最多准备两种替代方案，这可是远远不够的，我总是完完整整地想好四五种应急方案。如果我觉得这样也不够时，比如在面对一场非常重要的博弈或者要紧的事情时，我会做出七八种方案以防万一。"

孙正义告诉孙泰藏，单一选项是根本不够的，其价值往往微不足道。要保证每件事情进展顺利，一般都应该准备四五种预案，在某种方案发挥不了应有的作用时，这些预案就会发挥作用，我们的工作余地也就更大。长期以来，他自己正是这么做才能防患于未然的。

孙泰藏坦白地说："说实话，我吃了一惊，一个人怎么可能做这么多预案呢？"但他还是非常理解哥哥的话，"我哥哥说得非常正确，无论冒着多大的风险挑战，都不能让困难'扼杀'了自己，也不能让自己承受无法东山再起的致命打击。"

孙正义的战略愿景可以用"孙孙兵法"中"风林火山海"五个字概括。"风林火山"四个字既是中国古代兵法家孙子著作中的内容，也是日本武将武田信玄的座右铭。

"风、林、火、山"四个字代表的是"疾如风，徐如林，攻如火,定如山",这是一种勇猛果敢的战斗法则。在此基础上,孙正义又加上了"海",意味着胜利后,企业应该像海洋一样包围着竞争对手和他们周围的一切。

武田信玄的竞争对手上杉谦信以犀利果决的战斗风格而闻名,但孙正义不一样,实际上他曾在一本杂志的特邀文章中写下过这样一段话:

"上杉谦信希望每场战斗都打得漂亮,他在不断探索着战斗的艺术和生命的意义。当然,很多人都觉得他的战斗充满了浪漫色彩,常常陶醉在他的战斗故事里。但就个人而言,为了赢得美誉和赞扬,在商业竞争中贸然出手,为取得戏剧性的胜利而从事成功率较低的新业务是完全没有必要的。"[①]

孙正义的理想作战策略是久经考验后形成的"不战而屈人之兵",意料之外亦是情理之中。制定一个精确的战略,让一切步入正轨,顺势发展,最后取得水到渠成的胜利。

孙泰藏解释说:"在步履维艰的情况下,做出生死抉择就是唯一的出路。在这样关键的时刻,信念决定了成败。信念的重要性是毫无疑问的,但是如果你每一次都让同伴陷入'生

---

① 本段摘自日本商务杂志《总裁》1997年1月刊《商界精英奉为座右铭的〈孙子兵法〉语录》一文。

死'抉择，总是让同伴倍感绝望，那么作为一位领导者，你便是彻底失败的。"

柳井正是日本迅销公司的董事长，他带领公司把日本服装公司优衣库打造成了全球品牌。1994年柳井正促成迅销公司上市，同年软银公司上市。孙正义认为他们俩才是志同道合的人，正因如此，柳井正现在已经是软银集团的外派董事了。

当柳井正第一次获悉愿景银行正借助计算机和局域网对公司运营实行日记账制度管理模式时，立即设法登门当面向孙正义请教这套日记账系统的操作方法。

日记账制度管理模式可以保障企业掌握包括销售额和利润在内的各种经营指标，使公司决策层更快地了解并处理各种突发情况。有了这些长期一贯的数据信息，管理者就可以做到对公司运营的一切情况洞若观火，如此一来，取得最终的成功也就是自然而然的事情，绝非奇迹或者好运使然。

"成功应该是干净利落、货真价实的，而不应是徒有其表、华而不实的。"

这是一位商界领袖说过的话，它准确无误地反映了孙正义商业战略的本质与核心。

风险与危险

你和我一样，都是冒险家。

——比尔·盖茨《未来之路》

这是微软公司创始人比尔·盖茨在他的书中对孙正义的评价。

孙正义认为比尔·盖茨对他的这句评价是他"最大的荣誉"，并为此感到非常自豪。

孙正义从弟弟孙泰藏的经历中非常清晰地获知了如何区别风险和危险。

"你唯一能控制和管理的危险是被称为'风险'的东西，这种风险往往潜伏在可预测的范围内、有可能给你带来最严重损失的地方，而其他没有被预测到的一切因素都是有危险的。"

因此，孙正义说："你可以承受风险，但是不能承受危险。"

在孙正义看来，危险的意思更接近于"危害"。风险和危害是一个人在商业活动中必须清楚了解并加以区分的事情。

比尔·盖茨也非常清楚这一点，所以，他称孙正义为真正的冒险家。

孙正义告诫大家，不要抱着孤注一掷的想法做决定，如果一个人没有能力估算到潜在风险和可能招致的损失到底是什么就贸然行动，在没有估算出最大损失的情况下，根据胜负的可能性来决定自己的行为，这只能算稍有谋略的做法，并不值得推崇。

"也许你可以凭借运气解决问题，但是做生意是要经过无数次商场较量的，如果按照这样的趋势发展下去，没有谋略注定无法取得最终的成功。这就是我认为经商不能冒险的原因。"

事实是，风险和危险之间的界限常常是模糊的，如果你不能对两者进行区分，那么你还能做些什么呢？

在不清楚是否存在风险或危险的情况下，你是会果断采取行动还是决定偃旗息鼓、静观事态的变化？是决定做而采取行动，还是决定不做而无所成就？孙正义会怎么选择呢？

孙正义不会让两者的界限含糊不清。他会尽力判断出这是风险还是危险。

孙泰藏说道："无论是对的方面，还是错的方面，他都会分析每一个未知的细节。"他已多次目睹过哥哥是如何解决这件事的。

孙正义会发现隐藏在风险和危险之间某个层次的界限，他不会轻易放手，而是坚持获得真正的答案。

这个过程就像是一个人盯着无数盏彩灯，慢慢分辨出哪些是红色的，哪些是绿色的。在孙正义成立他的第一家公司之前，为了从庞杂的市场调查数据信息中得出结论，他会把对应领域的专业人士请到福冈，向他们支付交通费，还有不菲的报酬。

目前，他常常通过电话咨询的方式请教他人解决问题的方法。

如果他觉得风险和危险之间的界限是模糊的，他会马上拿起电话，不管什么时间，就开始给别人打电话，比如："你好，杰克！"

杰克是中国企业家马云。

"我觉得，马云可能也是终日忙得不可开交，但哥哥还是会一如既往地向这些行业翘楚咨询。"孙泰藏笑道。

"我想问你一个问题。"这是孙正义拿起电话后常说的第一句话。

在这种关键时刻，孙正义打电话请教的人都是各个领域的顶级人士，这是他的原则和一贯做法。不仅现在如此，在他成为顶级商人之前，也是这么做的。孙正义从顶级人士那里获得相关领域的最新信息，之后确定有关的行动是仅存在风险，还是会招致危险。对这个问题，他从不含糊。

孙正义非常有才华，这种才华表现在他可以在判断风险和危险这件事中，通过非常谨慎、深思熟虑的分析，得出一个商业战斗中的"最大损失估值"，而这种最大损失估值可能是很多人闻所未闻的。正如他所说，一旦能估算出最大的可能损失，它就不再是一种危险，我们可以采取措施及时止损，这样，危险就变成了风险。然而，这并不是一个普通人能够做到的。

"我还是不明白。"如果有人觉得这听起来有些模棱两可，孙正义会一遍又一遍地对周围的人解释他的思想。

他就是用自己敏锐而坚忍的意志将"危险"转为"风险"。

"一流攻守群"

我们要心甘情愿地为自己心中的美好憧憬奉献一切。既然已经决定把一生都付之于此，就不能毫无章法地行动，你必须拥有一个战略。

那么这个战略应该是怎样的呢？

孙正义的回答是五个字——"一流攻守群"，这也是孙正义"孙孙兵法"的25个字中的5个。

"一"

"一"在日本汉字中是"第一"的意思，表达了"成为第一"的决心。

孙正义对"第一"有一种特别的执着。

"小学的时候，我几乎都是第一名，如果不是第一名，我就会感到非常不自在。"他解释道，"当然，我从来没想过在音乐上要成为第一名，因为我有点五音不全。"

"但是，在我认为自己能抢占先机的领域，我就绝对要成为第一名，并且要遥遥领先于他人。"

"你必须先找到成为第一名的办法，再着手为进入这个领域做准备——要做就做压倒性的第一名。"

"如果你是第二名，就是失败的。"

"如果只是第二名，你怎么能成事呢？没有远大的志向，就只会甘于平庸，随声附和。"

但是，成为第一名并不是孙正义的最终目的。

"只有成为压倒性的第一名，你才能感受这一地位存在的本质意义。"

"你成了第一名，就会有更广阔的平台，更有利于挑战新事物、开发新技术，更能明白如何以客户的需求为出发点。我所希望的是，能够为这个世界承担起一份责任。"

所以他露出宽厚的笑容对别人说："在任何领域成为第一都是一种非常美妙的体验。"

"流"

"流"这个字在日本汉字中是"流动"的意思,表示应该认清时代的潮流价值取向。

"总是提前想半步,一步,或者三步,不断做出预判,同时拟定策略。"

"我正为之努力的目标是瞄准中心的中心。"

"不要把简单的事情复杂化。作为一名企业家,如果刻意选择逆流而上,自行其是,那么他就不是一名成功的企业家。倒行逆施的行为和商业格格不入。"

"你必须选择合适的对手、合适的市场,这种选择本身就是非常重要的决策。"

"董事长决定公司将涉足的主要经营领域。"

"一"和"流"组合起来,意味着"出类拔萃"。

"攻"

"攻"这个字在日本汉字中是进攻的意思,表达的思想是不勇敢面对挑战是不对的。

"如果仅完成常规的工作,你就无法迎来期待中的改变。"

那么对企业家来说,什么是"攻"呢?

"掌握大量技术，具备无与伦比的销售能力，拥有不可思议的谈判技能。"

孙泰藏所著的《孙正义论》一书中完整地展示了孙正义商业能力的实质性表现。

"有人对我说，孙正义看起来更像是一个风投基金合伙人，而不是一家公司的董事长。这是一种错误的认识，但从某些角度来说又有一定的道理。"

事实上，孙正义已经制订并实施了许多大规模收购项目计划，在风险投资方面，他表现出色。

然而，另一方面，作为一名企业家，他不断积累的知识经验和认知能力能让他获得创造新事物的可能性，而且这种可能性很大。

作为一名商人，他在日本各地建设网络基础设施、运营门户网站、管理电子商务等方面取得了成功。作为一名职业投资人，这让他具备了可以非常准确地评估任何企业价值的能力。

孙泰藏谈及孙正义的能力时说："他有一种任何人都无法比拟的能力，他可以同时通过技术参数和金融因素两个方面评估科技的发展，借助这种评估，他可以预测行业的未来发展趋势。从这个角度讲，说他是'全球最佳风险投资家'也不为过。"

"守"

"守"这个字在日本汉字中有"防守"的意思,"守"的对象通常是资本或者货币。

"大多数初创企业的失败都是因为现金流或者与现金流相关的环节出现了问题。"

"只有获得足够的资金,企业才能持续发动攻势。"

"务必确保公司在保持攻势的同时现金周转正常。"

"我们要做到攻守兼备,让二者相得益彰。"

"同时,我们要严格遵守法律法规,决不能做任何违背公平和正义的事。"

"群"

"群"是集体的意思。

不依赖某一个体,无论是一件产品、一个人,还是单一的商业领域。

"我们要有意识地实现多样化和异质化。"

我们的目标是打造战略性协作的企业生态系统,实施多个品牌、多种商业模式的群体合作战略。

"单一品牌、单一商业模式不可能支撑一家企业维持并发展300年。"

雅虎日本、阿里巴巴、亚马逊……与这些志同道合的一流公司群策群力、共同协作才能成就自己。实际上，软银集团本身就是一个独立分散且兼顾协调合作的企业集团。

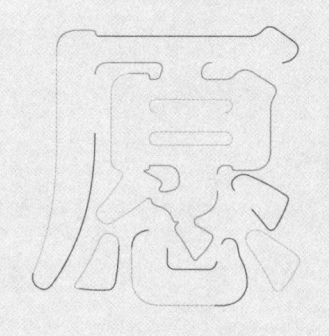

第五章
言行一致

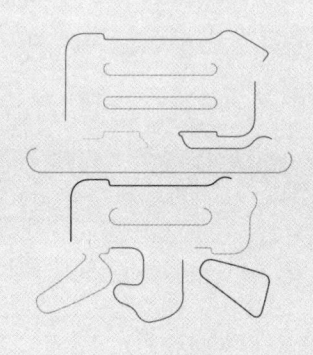

我将永远恪守承诺

那是在 2005 年,孙正义递给史蒂夫·乔布斯一张他画的草图,上面是他的一个设想——一款能够当手机使用的音乐播放器(iPod)。

"正义,我不需要你的图纸,我已经有我的想法了。"

这件事情发生在苹果手机发布的两年之前,但是,在乔布斯的脑海中,已经绘制好了苹果手机(iPhone)未来的样子。即便如此,孙正义也没有灰心气馁。

"那你的产品一旦完成,请一定把它的在日销售代理权给我。"

孙先生希望乔布斯在产品发布后,把在日销售权给他。

"正义，你疯了！我都还没有和任何人谈过产品的研发呢。"乔布斯满脸震惊地说道，"但是，我会把这款产品在日本的销售代理权给你，因为你是第一个找我谈的人。"

"如果你能恪守承诺，那么届时我将会是你在日本的运营商。"

在 2006 年，孙先生以 155 亿美元收购了英国沃达丰公司的日本分公司——日本沃达丰电信公司。如今的通信公司日本软银就是这样发展而来的。

当然，他们并没有签署过任何合同。但是他们都知道，这份承诺比任何书面合同都更具分量。

2011 年 10 月 5 日，乔布斯逝世，享年 56 岁。得知此消息后，孙正义立即发表声明，表示沉痛哀悼。

"伯牙绝弦，再无知音。乔布斯是当代的奇才，他在艺术和科技领域建树斐然，几百年后，当人们回看乔布斯的一生，会认为他与莱昂纳多·达·芬奇一样伟大。他的成就将永远铭刻在人们的心中。"

2013 年 10 月 21 日，在乔布斯去世两年后，孙先生又失去了一位对他而言无可替代的朋友——笠井和彦（享年 76 岁）。

笠井和彦努力勤恳，凭借自己的工作能力，逐步升迁为日本一家大银行的主席。他在 63 岁时应孙先生的诚恳邀请，成为软银集团的总监。他始终力挺孙先生。即使是在互联网泡沫破灭、软银股价跌至过去的百分之一的时候，又或是在非对称数字用户线路（ADSL）业务连续 4 年损失数百亿日元之时，甚至是在孙先生戏剧性地做出收购沃达丰公司的决定之时，他都一如既往地支持着孙先生。

笠井和彦和孙先生之间只发生过一次激烈的争执。那时，雷曼兄弟公司破产引发的混乱刚刚平息下来，软银公司的业绩正在慢慢回升。

在悼念笠井和彦的时候，孙正义说道："我个人认为，股市波动会令投资者紧张焦虑，而向分析师和新闻记者解释这些变化会非常无聊。所以我和他说：'我觉得也许我们应该走私有化路线，我个人可以对公司负责。'他打断我，说道：'我决不同意。'"

笠井和彦对孙正义说："公司现在确实运行得很顺利，所以我们可以回到以前私人所有的模式，我们能获得所需的资源，并想出解决这些问题的办法。但这真的是你想要的吗？软银需要走出去，走出日本，走向世界，变得更加强大。难道你真的仅仅因为事情烦琐复杂，就要让我们的梦想大打折扣吗？"

回想起和彦的话，孙正义说道："现在，再去想他所说的话，我才意识到，如果当初和彦没有阻止我，我们很有可能无法买下美国的斯普林特公司，之后也不可能实现这么大的梦想。"

自那之后，孙正义一直把这句话铭记于心。

"我将恪守承诺。"

笠井和彦总是支持孙正义及他那无限的雄心，正是出于这个原因，每当孙正义做出任何阻碍或限制自己梦想的决定时，他都会强烈地反对。而孙正义也完全理解他的良苦用心。

这份承诺就是与人类分享一个伟大梦想，这份承诺也是对自己的承诺。

即使到现在，孙正义也没有忘记这份承诺，他会永远恪守承诺、履行承诺。

我的发际线没有后移，只不过是我在不断前行

2013年1月8日，孙正义发布了这样一条推文：

"我的发际线没有后移，只不过是我在不断前行。"

这条推文是孙正义对另外一条推文的回应，因为有人发推文开玩笑地说他的发际线正在"急剧后退"。他这条机智的回应被转发了4万多次，并得到了不少好评和笑脸。

实际上，孙正义的确是在不断前进，他通过一系列大规模收购活动，加快了自己前进的步伐。

1995年，他以约800亿日元收购了世界上最大的计算机博览会COMDEX的销售部门。1996年，他以约2 100亿日元的价格收购了世界上最大的与计算机相关的文献出版公司——齐夫－戴维斯出版公司。他一共投资了大概2 900亿日元，而软银的企业市值，在1994年首次公开募股后为2 700亿日元，低于孙正义的总投资额。也就是说，他在36岁时完成了公司上市，而且在接下来两年里相继完成了上面所说的这些大规模交易。正如孙正义所说："我已经获得了驶向世界的地图和指南针。"

2006年，软银集团以大约1.75万亿日元的价格收购了英国沃达丰日本公司。此次对电信运营商的成功收购让孙正义获得了苹果手机的在日独家销售权，因此公司的签约数也得到了大幅提升。2013年，他以大约1.8万亿日元的价格收购了美国电信公司斯普林特公司——全球互联网骨干网服务商、美国第三大长途电话公司。同年，他又以大约3.3万亿日元的价格收购了英国ARM公司，这是一家英国的半导体设计公司，是全球领先的半导体知识产权提供商，全世界超过95%的智能手机和平板电脑都采用ARM的架构。

关于孙正义发际线的讨论仍在继续，甚至愈演愈烈。2013年10月8日，在发布那条"前进"推文的9个月之后，孙正义看到了一篇关于《软银与其竞争对手之间赤裸裸且毫无意义的价格战》的文章。"我还没有秃呢，我头上还有头发。"他在推特上回复道。他的另一条推文写道："秃头不是病，是男人的象征。"

2012年诺贝尔生理学或医学奖获得者山中伸弥，也曾就秃头问题开过玩笑。在诺贝尔奖颁奖典礼上，京都大学教授、京都大学物质－细胞统合系统据点iPS细胞研究所所长山中伸弥对共同获奖者约翰·格登的评论引来阵阵笑声。

"我对您的一切都钦佩不已，包括您的头发。"

"我非常欣赏您聪慧的脑袋，内在丰富的知识和外在浓密的头发。"

孙正义和山中伸弥的共同之处，不仅仅是这一点。

山中伸弥的父亲是小镇上一家小工厂的经理，与孙正义一样，他从小受父亲的影响，看着父亲自力更生、独立创业。他长大后成了一名医生，因为父亲对他说过，他不适合管理，不要选择从事商业。然而，山中伸弥现在是他所在研究所的所长，在通过众筹等方式获取资金方面，他已成为同行中的佼佼者。

孙正义16岁时去了美国，亲身经历了加利福尼亚那片蓝天下的"自我解放"运动。山中伸弥在1993年获得博士学位后，继续出国深造，30岁时在美国加利福尼亚大学旧金山分校下属的格拉德斯通研究所攻读博士后。

在那里，他全身心地投入研究，这为他后来的研究奠定了基础。山中伸弥称自己是一个不称职的医生，但他发现自己可以在这个新的环境中作为一名研究者不断绽放光彩。加利福尼亚这片蓝天下似乎真的蕴藏着特别的、奇妙的力量。

然而，山中伸弥在海外学习期间所收获的不止于此。

VW，即"愿景"和"努力"。他从他的老师罗伯特·马利那里了解到，这两者是成功的要诀，不仅适用于研究，也适用于生活。直到今天，这依旧是山中伸弥的座右铭。

孙正义和山中伸弥都为了在世界舞台上实现各自的梦想而不懈奋斗。但这并不意味着他们为人古板严肃。这两个人也充满了幽默感，有时也会逗得大家笑个不停。他们带来的欢笑不仅打动人心，还是他们实现梦想的伟大力量。此外，他们还分别担任了孙正义育英基金会（财团）的主席和副主席。

我宁愿做硅谷

2014年3月11日，孙正义在美国一档著名的电视访谈节目中接受查理·罗斯的采访时,聊起了他对日本传奇企业家的敬佩之情。

"你心目中的偶像是本田公司的本田宗一郎先生和索尼公司的盛田昭夫先生吗?"查理·罗斯问道。查理是当时美国最著名的电视节目主持人之一。

孙正义转向观众,说道:"因为本田公司的本田先生和索尼公司的盛田先生都富有激情、眼光卓绝,而且他们都是大品牌的创始人;他们作为先驱者,一位引领了日本汽车产业,另一位引领了日本电子产业的发展,在没有政府扶持的情况下,凭借一己之力,对抗已有的产业巨头,所以他们都是我的偶像。"

查理·罗斯接着提了一个别有深意的问题。

"那你是不是更像一位金融工程师,既知道如何做交易,又知道如何找到你想要与之交易的公司,而不是一个富有创造力的人呢?"

罗斯口中所说的"金融工程师",可能指的是策划投资的人,即专业投资人士。孙正义听出了话里的讽刺意味,巧妙地运用了一则简单的暗喻回答他。

"如果史蒂夫·乔布斯代表的是艺术和科技,那么我就是金融和科技。"

"而非艺术?"查理·罗斯惊讶地问道。也许这样的回答很罕见，因为很少有企业家会宣称自己不是艺术家。

"我喜欢艺术，但是我不是艺术家，于我而言，信息革命——为人类创造新的生活方式，才是更重要的事情。"

"如果我可以为人类带来信息革命，那么我并不需要任何事情都亲力亲为，因为我可以借助其他人的才能，而我只负责建设好基础设施就可以了。我没有必要去制造法拉利或本田汽车，但我可以为所有优秀的汽车建造一条高速公路。我可以为汽车革命建造收费站，甚至是整个生态系统。"

"这是我正在努力的事业，我想要为大家带来信息革命。"

孙正义先前就曾提到，虽然日本在互联网技术领域处于领先地位，但是其基础设施（即"高速公路"）相对匮乏。

"所以我选择挑战日本电报电话公司，该公司成立于1976年，是日本最大的电信服务提供商、日本电信电话公社的全资子公司。该公司占日本'信息高速公路'的市场份额达99%。"

当罗斯问及孙正义的谈判哲学是什么时，孙正义的回答恰如其分且自信满满。

"我总是向前看，不留恋过去，不贪恋眼下。如果我们有更大的力量，未来10年、20年，我们能做些什么呢？什么会让你感到激动不已？

"信息革命是唯一让我愿意为之奋斗终生的事业，人类经历了农业革命、工业革命,而现在正面临着第三次革命——信息革命。这项进步意义非凡,在未来300年它将一直延续下去。正因如此我们才有了300年的愿景,我们才想要专注于信息革命。"孙正义回答道。

接下来的谈话,让孙正义骄傲地宣称自己"不是艺术家"的原因变得更加明了。他还反对如今很多企业固有的零和博弈的思想。

"我并不在乎这些科技是否由我们和我们的雇员发明创造。"他说道,"我所关心的是如何把每个人的奇思妙想融入我们的生态系统。

"许多美国公司只对一个品牌感兴趣,相信只要有一种商业模式就能征服世界。

"我不是那种人。我对合作深信不疑,我们公司旗下也有很多合资企业。我会决定向哪些企业家投资,努力帮助他们发展他们热爱的事业。如果我有能力帮助所有这些优秀的企业家,那么我们一定会创造出伟大的科技和优质的服务。这些就是让我最开心的事情。

"我不需要成为英雄,我更愿意成为我们创建的整个生态系统里的一个英雄。那是我的一个300年的愿景,我不愿把自己束缚在一款产品、一种商业模式、一个品牌之中。"

当科技进步成为你的第一要务,你就没有必要当一名艺术家了。孙正义能够利用自己的金融实力支持那些艺术家型的企业家,从而激发他们的热忱,助力其走向成功。这就是孙正义的想法。

从这层意义上来看,孙正义的创业立场显然与本田和索尼这样的公司相左。这种观念上的改变可能是孙正义带给日本公司最伟大的模式创新。

正如孙正义说的那样:"我宁愿做硅谷。"

这种想法远远超出了在硅谷创建一家企业或一个社区的范畴,他说话时的激情彰显了他对自己成为硅谷生态系统的渴望。

放飞自我,自由飞翔!

2016年12月5日,孙正义利用私人资金创立了孙正义育英基金会。他任命2012年诺贝尔生理学或医学奖得主、京都大学教授山中伸弥为副主席。董事包括东京大学的校长五神真,顾问包括职业将棋棋士羽生善治。

他将建立基金会的目的宣布如下:

"为有远大抱负、才华横溢的青年提供一个能够提升他们技能,改善人类未来的环境。"

孙正义讨厌一道名为幕之内便当（一种典型的日式便当，其中有米饭和几种不同的配菜）的日本菜。有一次，当他的秘书正要出门为他买午餐的时候，他甚至对秘书说："千万别买幕之内便当，拜托了！"

这倒不是因为他对食物很挑剔，他只是希望便当里的内容能够清清楚楚，如猪肉便当里就是猪肉、鱼肉便当里就是鱼肉、中式便当里就是中国菜。对他来说，最好的方案就是从多种不同的便当中选择出最特别的。这些便当不需要非常有名，他从不在乎品牌。

有一次我在与孙正义先生会面时，给他带了一件礼物。这件礼物不是铜锣烧，而是在市中心一家小点心店买的虎纹烧。之所以叫虎纹烧，是因为这种点心经过烘焙以后会呈现虎皮一样的纹路。这种日式点心是由一对老夫妻在一间小厨房里制作而成的，味道鲜美而质朴，风味独特，孙正义先生就喜欢吃这类美食。

后来在庆祝公司成立 30 周年时，我决定不送孙先生虎纹烧了，而是送他红白馒头（红白相间的馒头，有吉祥之意）。我让他们把数字 30 印在馒头上。然而当我收到成品时，简直目瞪口呆。也许他们从来没有做过这种带有题字的点心纪念品，因此印在上面的数字非常粗糙，一看就是经验不足。然而孙先生却非常喜欢。这馒头味道不错,但印在上面的数字显然写得不好。他盯着馒头,似乎在欣赏这种笨拙,并像往常一样非常有礼貌地感谢我。

他对人也是如此。

孙正义育英基金会旨在资助才华横溢的年轻人。2019年7月11日,基金会资助了187位年龄为8~28岁的年轻人。将各个领域的优秀人才聚集在一起,涉及机器人技术、编程、数学、物理、科学、文学及艺术等。

2018年12月26日,在孙正义育英基金会年度报告会上,孙正义发表了一场激励人心的讲话。

"我16岁去美国,眼前看到的一切,让我深受激励。周遭环境截然不同。与操着不同口音、怀有不同想法的人打交道,真的能够激发整个大脑。你们这群年轻人,个个才华横溢,当你们每天在一起生活、一起工作、一起度过你们的岁月时,你们必将相互启发、相互促进、更上一层楼。你们要开阔眼界、创造机遇、成长成熟、造福四方。"

他所做的就是为拥有卓越才能的人创建一个相互交流、共同创造的平台。

"日本的教育旨在把每个人提高至'平均'水平。而美国和中国则不同,它们正在实行一种旨在发掘和培养高精尖人才独特才能的教育体系。我的工作就是帮助培养这部分杰出人才，未来他们对日本的发展将至关重要，他们将是日本未来的领导者。"孙正义说道。

孙正义上小学时的梦想是成为一名老师，然而，当时由于种种原因，包括家族背景问题，他放弃了这个梦想。

2017年2月10日，在一次孙正义育英基金会活动之后，我问孙正义对年轻人有什么寄语。

"在任何领域，解放自我、自由翱翔！这就是我想告诉他们的。"孙正义注视着这些天才，仿佛看到了他们的未来，两眼如星般闪耀。

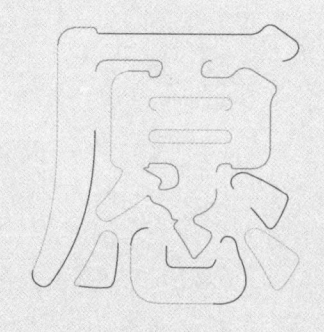

第六章
技术进化论

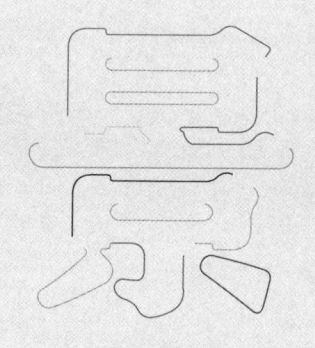

洞悉时代潮流

2019年2月6日,在公司2018财年第三季度盈收结果简报会上,孙正义阐述了他对愿景的看法。

"我一提到'愿景'二字,你们可能会想到一些浪漫的东西,比如一场梦或一个幻想,总之,都是一些朦朦胧胧、不切实际的事物。"

孙正义可不是这么想的,他说:"我个人认为,愿景是一种摆在你们面前的挑战,是非常清晰、富有逻辑、极其确定的东西。"

但是,如果你想让自己眼中的愿景清晰透彻、符合实际,那么你就有必要清晰而准确地了解这个时代及其发展变迁情况。

孙正义邀请所有观众一起回顾软银集团40年的发展历史，他宣称，自成立以来，公司每天都在做一件事情，并将继续做下去。这件事就是推动信息革命。

"信息革命的浪潮大约每10年就会兴起一次，它们往往会引起一波接一波的颠覆性社会变革。信息革命是一种大规模的革命，这种规模的革命往往是几百年才发生一次，在这场革命的漫长的推进过程中，大约每10年就可能孕育一段上升期。"

他回顾了信息革命的历史，将其分为几个阶段，一一向观众介绍说明。他说："一开始是集成电路的时代，后来诞生了个人计算机，再接着软银集团成立了，然后互联网、宽带、智能手机走进了人们的生活。这些根本性的转变和进步，大约每10年发生一次。现在，我认为我们面临的是最大的根本性变革——人工智能革命。我相信人工智能革命将是信息革命中最重大的根本性转变。"

即使孙正义认为愿景应该是非常清晰、符合逻辑且确定的，但他也明白愿景不是平白无故突然出现在人们大脑中的东西。他认为："这是你每天每时每刻都要思考的事情，一直到你的头脑完全被'拧干'为止，这不是只需要经过两三天思考，就会灵光乍现的事情。"

换句话说，能够精准捕捉时代变迁的愿景不会是模棱两可的。相反，它需要以一种明确的方式，即通过漫长而深远的思考，来捕捉那些时代的变革。

不管面对来自任何国家的任何一位青年创造者，在他们的创业初期，孙正义总是这样对他们说：

"你要洞察时代变迁，放眼未来的发展。挑战自己，做到领先时代半步、一步、两步、三步的事，然后在那里等待。"

"把你的商业轴心放在朝阳产业，而非大势已去的夕阳产业里。"

"洞悉时代潮流。"

"洞悉时代潮流，你才会看到未来。"

"你越是不笃定，就越需要看得更远。"

寻找下一个马云

2015年10月，软银金融研究院举办的学术专题讲座，实际上是孙正义与尼克什·阿罗拉（时任软银集团代表董事、总裁）的一场交流对话。这场学术讲座旨在培养下一代企业家，其中就包括孙正义的继任者。

软银集团一直都在寻找年轻的初创企业创始人，并为他们的激情和创造力投资，而且把这项工作作为一种商业战略。尼克什对此赞叹不已。

尼克什还曾预言:"这些企业家中有 5~10 个将会是下一个埃隆·马斯克,史蒂夫·乔布斯,或者拉里·佩奇,所以软银集团将成为企业家的投资组合公司。"

随着前几代企业家走向成熟,软银集团将年青一代初创企业创始人纳入其投资组合。软银集团尽其所能向年青一代创业者提供资金和资源帮助,同时,还组建了包含一些成熟企业和初创企业创始人的"家庭网",这些企业能够为初创企业提供各种支持,同时还能提供指导和开设创业课程。尼克什激情澎湃地说:"这正是孙正义为中国企业家马云所做过的事情。"

他接着问孙正义:"你是怎么找到这些人的?世界上有这么多企业,你选择的标准是什么?在上一轮的搜索中,我发现处于初创阶段的企业多达 150 万家。然而你还是找到了马云。你是怎么找到这些人并让他们加入软银家族的?"

世界上每一个初创企业创始人都想知道这个问题的答案。孙正义回答说:"是的,我们必须创造一套体系并借助它来实现这一点。"

孙正义不想凭借个人判断来完成这项任务。相反,他想创建一套体系,让企业本身就能够发现大有前途的初创企业创始人。

"我们需要某种体系来识别所有早期初创企业中更具活力的企业和更富创造性的创始人。我们还需要通过一种体系来筛选这些初创企业的创始人。我们通过筛查选择足够大的企业，然后放弃小企业，即优胜劣汰、择优选取。当剩下的大企业发展得更加强大时，我们就要决定该投资哪家企业，不该投资哪家企业。"

孙正义给大家讲了一个非常著名的案例，说的是1999年他是如何在5分钟内闪电般地做出决定，向马云投资2 000万美元的事情。后来孙正义解释说："当我看到他的眼神时，我就知道我们是同一类人。"

然而，这可能并不是事情的全部，孙正义不会过多讲述他内心的想法。最有可能的是，在1999年那个决定性的时刻到来之前，他已经准备了许久，已经做过透彻的研究和分析，并且创造了自己的一套能够识别像马云这样的企业家的系统。

传感器、三叶虫和寒武纪大爆发

2016年10月，ARM公司的年度技术会议在硅谷的中心——加利福尼亚州圣何塞举行。这次会议是在软银集团收购ARM公司之后不久举行的，ARM是英国的一家主要从事半导体设计、拥有大量智力资产的全球性实体公司。

孙正义向众人提问:"地球上第一类长眼睛的物种是什么?"他停顿了一会儿,然后继续说:"是三叶虫。"

他想说明什么呢?

眼睛是终极传感器。回顾所有生物的起源,你会发现因为拥有眼睛这一"传感器",三叶虫很快超越了其他各种生物诞生和进化的速度。孙正义说,这对我们现代社会来讲同样意义深远。

"如今,我们可以将最新的技术安装到我们的物联网中。有了这项最新技术,你可以将传感器安装在物联网上,让它们进行信息识别、深度学习及推理,并且驱动传感器不断运转。这个循环和动物物种的进化是一样的。从这种意义上讲,寒武纪大爆发和物联网技术的大爆发本质上是一回事。"

他的意思是物联网时代的"三叶虫"才刚刚诞生。

现在,许多采用最新技术制造的物联网设备都配有传感器。因此,很多东西都"长眼睛"了。

传感器使"识别"所有的发明创造成为可能。孙正义最推崇的理论之一就是:基于认知的推理是人类进化到现在这种程度的原因。例如,人类是如何"识别"天空中飞行的鸟、推演并最终创造出适宜飞行的机器的形状和结构的。

大数据和深度学习使各种配备传感器的物体能够识别并推算出由它们的"眼睛"捕捉到的大量现象。

因此无机物开始像生物一样进化。

这就是孙正义对未来的愿景。

期盼奇点①

现如今，计算机在国际象棋、围棋和天气预报等方面已经变得比人类智能得多。在未来 30 年，它们会发展得更加智能。这是我们人类刚刚开始接受的新现实。

2017 年 10 月 1 日，孙正义在投资者大卫·鲁宾斯坦的电视节目中提出了一个理论并列举了一些事实，似乎与这一信念相悖。

孙正义的英语演讲，正如他的日语演讲一样直截了当，只涉及要点。"ARM 公司拥有 99% 的市场份额。"他开始说道。

软银集团于 2016 年收购了 ARM 公司，几乎完全掌控了移动微处理器的设计技术，而这些微处理器被称为计算机的

---

① 奇点，是指技术，尤其是在人工智能方面，所有的进步将会带来智能化程度比人类还要高的机器的时间点。孙正义预测，超级智能机器会在 2047 年之前迎来曙光。

"大脑"。

"20年后,它们将能够运送1万亿块芯片,设计1万亿块芯片。这个星球上没有人可以离开这些芯片而生存。它们存在于任何地方——车里、冰箱里……如果每个人都需要这些芯片,而一家公司拥有它99%的市场份额,那么这家公司的价值将不可估量。"

然而,有些人感受到了来自这种价值观的威胁,更具体地说,他们害怕某一天,机器人将变得如此智能,它们将彻底毁灭人类。大卫·鲁宾斯坦针对这种恐惧向孙正义发问。

"这种风险当然存在。"孙正义承认道,然后他以一种更乐观的语调,继续回答,"但是如果你回顾人类的历史,你会发现人们在无数次战斗中互相厮杀。但是今天,我们的日常生活中不再存在那些野蛮行为,我们变得更文明了。所以当科技发展进化到了超级机器人智能远远超过人类智能的时候,我们就会明白战争不是一件好事,总体而言,和谐共存才是对社会更好的选择。"

孙正义对此深信不疑。

"机器人为我们着想,帮助我们,它们会让我们更快乐,于是我们有了更多的空间去爱彼此。"

当被问到"世界上什么东西会带给你最大的快乐"时,孙正义回答说:"我对即将到来的奇点有一个清晰的构想。"

他说,一想到他和他的投资组合公司将会帮助人类建设一个更加美好的世界,他就无比开心;一想到奇点通过规避意外事故、消除疾病,保护人们免于悲伤,使人们在未来生活得更好,他就无比开心;一想到他可以与其他人携手,共同实现这一伟大梦想,他就无比开心。孙正义坚信解决这些问题将会造福人类,这就是为什么他对奇点的到来感到如此兴奋。

孙先生的话清晰明确,坚定有力。

"接下来仍有许多工作要做。但是像这样特别的工作会创造无数机会。从这层意义上讲,困难可以被看作一种优势。这绝对是精彩的人生,而我乐在其中。"

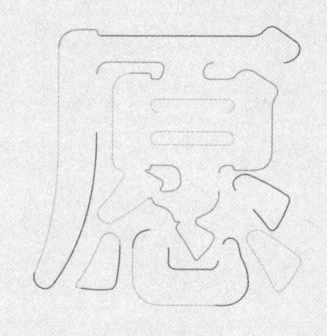

第七章
献给将与人工智能共存的人类

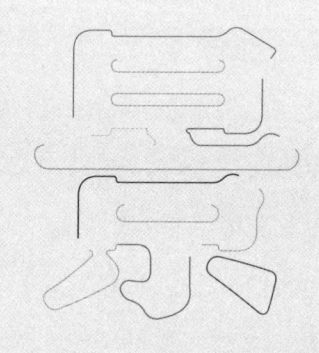

要像年轻的绝地武士一样

2019年3月,大卫·费伯采访孙正义时,问道:"你觉得你有能力左右科技的发展方向吗?"

孙先生道:"我只是很高兴能参与其中。"

他继续激动地说道:"没有我,一切仍然会发生。但是我愿意支持那些心中有梦、激情四射的创业者。科技发展非常迅猛,我很乐意做他们的协助者或支持者。"

孙先生还提到,在过去的30年间,工业部门发生了三次重大变革。

首先是在计算机中央处理器中增加了晶体管的数量,其次是扩大了其内存容量,最后是提高了通信速度。前两个是过去的 100 万倍，而第三个已是过去的 300 多万倍。

这对科技以及我们的生活方式都产生了巨大影响。如果这些变革继续发展，那么功率提高 100 多万倍的中央处理器将配备的内存容量也会是以前的 100 万倍，并且还能拥有达到过去 300 多万倍的通信速度。由此可以预见，这一定会带来巨大的改变。

计算机的强大功能使人工智能技术的普及成为现实。人工智能技术所具备的处理大量数据和进行预测的能力让我们有可能创造一个拥有智能机器人的未来。

正当孙先生畅谈未来时，出于记者的职业习惯，费伯评论道："我知道这一直是你投资的重点。"他的意思是，对于正在投资人工智能的孙先生来说，谈论他的人工智能梦想是有经济意义的。费伯继续问道："我记得你说过，人工智能将成为人类历史上最伟大的革命。"

孙正义回答道："是的。"

费伯："比以往的一切都要伟大吗？"

孙正义："伟大得多。"

费伯："你也曾说过你想将软银集团建设成为对人类发展贡献最大的集团。"

孙正义："没错。"

费伯:"你有信心实现这一梦想吗?"

孙正义:"我会竭尽全力。"

费伯:"具体怎么做呢?"

孙正义:"我将为那些进入该领域的新生力量提供帮助。在我看来,那些年轻的创业者就像是《星球大战》系列电影里的绝地武士一般,心中有梦,昂扬向上。"

孙先生认为,大学毕业后就直接开始创业的年轻人就像是"年轻的绝地武士"。

"这些年轻的'绝地武士'还在学习如何起飞,而事实上,其中一些聪颖者已经开始飞翔了。看着他们创造新的生活方式,解决人类面对的众多难题,不禁让人感到欣慰。"

在孙正义看来,这些"年轻的绝地武士"有能力找到治愈绝症的方案、减少事故发生的方法,有能力从整体上消除当今世界的低效问题,消除痛苦与悲伤。

然而,孙先生也清楚地知道,许多"年轻的绝地武士"会在这漫漫创业路上挣扎、失败。创办一家企业且有所成就绝不是一件容易的事情。但是,孙先生也一定看到了,尽管未来他们会遭受伤痛和苦难,但他们会再次站起来,以更强大的姿态重返战场。

人工智能将重新定义所有行业

2019年2月6日,孙正义在软银集团盈收结果简报会上发表讲话。他讲述了人工智能革命。

首先,他向观众陈述了现状。

"10年前,能进入全球十大企业的互联网企业只有1家。而如今,在短短10年的时间里,互联网企业就占据了全球前10排行榜中的7席。"

根据全球企业市值排行榜,我们会发现微软是2009年唯一入围全球十大企业的科技企业。经过快速发展,到了2019年,苹果与其他7家美国及中国的互联网企业同时跻身这份榜单之中。

也就是说,互联网发生了根本性变革。这就是迄今为止信息革命的成果。

然而,孙先生预言,人工智能将会主导信息革命的未来。他说:"几年后,在全球十大企业中人工智能企业将占据一半以上的席位。"这是为什么呢?

"这些在全球十大企业中占了7席的互联网企业具体重新定义了哪些行业呢?"孙正义说道,"简单来说,就两个行业:广告业和零售业。互联网重新定义的就是这两大行业。"

脸书和谷歌重塑了广告业的商业模式,从传统媒体那里抢走了消费者。亚马逊和阿里巴巴利用电子商务重塑了零售业的商业模式,从传统零售模式中夺走了顾客。

其实,人工智能带来的根本性变革所产生的影响将远大于目前互联网带来的根本性变革所产生的影响。人工智能必然会重新定义整个汽车行业的权力关系,同时也包括所有其他行业,从交通运输业,到教育、医药、房地产、金融业等。

孙正义还预言道:"人工智能将重新定义所有行业。"

他重复着这一理论的核心观点。在过去的30年里,中央处理器的晶体管数量增加了,内存容量扩大了,通信速度提高了。前两个都是过去的100万倍,而第三个已是过去的300多万倍。他笃信,在未来的30年间,这些数字还会持续增长。

"有史以来,人类第一次成功创造了比人类大脑运作更佳的人工智能。这些形式的人工智能具有自学能力。它们不需要人类手把手教它们,而是通过一系列输入过程自行感知数据,包括物联网、移动设备、汽车和建筑物等,并利用数据进行推断,根据数据得出结论。它们将重新定义许多行业。这就是我对未来的憧憬。"

孙先生对人类发展持乐观态度。他用简单明了却又恰到好处的类比阐述了这一观点。

"人类看见鸟儿在天空翱翔,就开始思考,要是人也能在空中飞翔该有多好呀，于是就有了达·芬奇制作的直升机原型。

"当哥白尼仰望星空时，他就开始思索，也许不是天空在移动，而是我们脚下的地球在转动。于是他提出了日心说，彻底改变了人们的思维方式。

"爱因斯坦看到光，提出了相对论，并写出'质能方程式'$E = mc^2$。

"换句话说，人类是通过观察、感知、推理而不断发展进步的。"

孙先生认为：推理是人类进步的最大源泉。

在人工智能革命中，人工智能将运用越来越强大的计算能力，对我们看到的和接触到的数据进行加工和推理。这就是人工智能革命为人类带来如此伟大进步的原因。

孙正义确信自己对这件事情的看法是完全正确的。

"人工智能必将重新定义所有行业，而这场人工智能革命才刚刚开始。"

误差，时差

2019年2月6日，在软银集团盈收结果简报会上，孙正义宣称："我认为再过几十年，纽约第五大道上将会挤满由人工智能控制的自动驾驶汽车。"他还说，这就和过去几十年间在第五大道上来回穿梭的马车被汽车取代是同一个道理。

至于"几十年"，他解释道："也许会提前 5 年，也许会推后 5 年。"

"但我个人认为，5 年或 10 年只是一点误差。重要的是发展的大方向。"

从马车到汽车是一次重大的根本性变革，而从由人类驾驶的汽车到由人工智能驾驶的汽车又是一次重大的根本性变革。

这是为什么呢？因为人工智能驾驶相比于人类驾驶更加安全。而计算机运行所需的三个要素，即中央处理器中晶体管的数量、内存容量和通信速度，即使到现在，仍在不断发展。

他有一个愿景，同时也有相应的逻辑解释。

"其他一切都只是误差。"

他喜欢"误差"这个词。

当天，孙正义在屏幕上展示了一个算式："25-4=9？"

"作为一家纯粹的控股公司，软银集团的股东价值就是我们控股的股权价值，25 万亿日元，减去 4 万亿日元的净债务，也就是 21 万亿日元。然而这一数字与其控股公司——软银集团——目前的市值之间存在近9万亿日元的巨大差距。"①

当有记者问及如何改变这种"差距"时,他不假思索地回答道:"这只是时差而已,交给时间吧,时间会做出评判的。"

鉴于软银集团承担了太多风险,而且债台高筑,于是有人提议应该削减它的企业价值。

"所有问题都会随着时间而消逝。到那时,就不会再有人有意见了。"

孙正义提到被誉为"奥马哈的先知"的沃伦·巴菲特投资过许多企业,根据"部分加总法"得出的这些企业的估值,现在是以溢价而不是折价来衡量的。

"快速发展的事物总有延迟效应。"他以玩笑的口吻,毫不犹豫地说道,"当我说'我的发际线没有后移,只不过是我在不断前行'时,大家都笑我,但是我真的一直在前进。"

他微微一笑,然后坚定地说道:"但我觉得人们对软银集团的评价会随着时间而改变。"

目前这只不过是误差和时差罢了。

---

① 文中所引用数据分别是截至2019年2月6日软银集团持有的股权价值,截至2018年底软银集团的净债务,以及截至2019年2月6日软银集团的市值。

"说大话"心态

日本现在缺少的正是"说大话"（obora mentality）的心态。日语中的"obora"一词带有否定的内涵，相当于汉语中的"吹牛"。但孙正义对之的理解却完全不同。若将他的理解翻译成汉语，这一词的意思则为"宏伟的愿景"。

2019年5月9日，孙先生在软银集团2018财年盈收结果简报会上宣布将开始筹建第二期软银愿景基金。该基金重点投资使用人工智能的领头企业，接受投资的企业往往都是全球各行业的佼佼者，其中就包括分别在美国和中国成功运营的共享出行企业优步和滴滴、印度本土的连锁酒店OYO等。其中许多都是独角兽企业（估值在10亿美元以上的初创企业），而孙先生则自称是"独角兽猎人"。

目前，这只致力于研究人工智能未来发展的基金被认为是软银集团"最大的经济增长来源"。在2019年6月29日的股东大会上，孙先生发布了他的宏伟目标：到2040年，集团总市值将达到200万亿日元。

有些人会嘲笑他的这个宏伟目标，认为这是在"说大话"。

"愿景基金不过是一个泡沫。"

"他为可能永远无法实现的利润投入太多了。"

"有息债务未免也太多了。"

孙正义全当这些批评是背景噪声。

"小时候,我就喜欢钓鱼。我知道撒更大的网,才能捕到更多鱼。"

在这场人工智能革命之前的互联网革命中,他错过了无数的投资机会。回望过去,他认为那是因为他没有足够的资金。他说:"这次,没有任何借口,我一定会抓住一切机会。"接着,孙正义先生继续讨论他的雄心壮志及宏伟蓝图。

"假如软银集团的投资总额为 6 万亿日元。[①] 如果基金的年增长率为 35%,那么 10 年后其价值将会是原来的 20 倍。如果保守一点估计,基金的年增长率为 26%,那么 10 年后其价值将会是原来的 10 倍,20 年后则达到 200 倍。再退一步,即使对所有方面都做保守估计,假如年增长率只有 19%,那么 20 年后其价值也可达 33 倍,从原来的 6 万亿日元变成 200 万亿日元。"

他曾说过他的梦想:"我们的市值要用万亿来计算。"但谁能想到会是 200 万亿呢?

[①] 截至 2019 年 9 月 6 日,软银集团对软银愿景基金的投资总额高达 331 亿美元(约 3.5 万亿日元)。

在2019年的股东大会上,软银集团播放了一段15年前召开股东大会的视频。那时候,孙先生才40多岁。他说:"我希望在我60多岁的时候,我们的净利润能够达到1万亿日元、2万亿日元。"接着,他不失幽默地脱口而出:"哎呀,这算是'说大话'吗?"这句话引起了观众的一片笑声。

那时候,正是公司连续4年亏损100亿日元之际。这也许是"说大话",但即便在当时,他也毫不掩饰他所渴望得到的东西。2018年,他已经61岁了,软银集团的净利润已经超过了1万亿日元。实际上,孙先生所讲的"说大话"就是一个"宏伟的愿景",一个他有能力实现的宏伟愿景。

我也许会后悔,但决不退缩

2019年11月6日,在软银集团召开的2019财年中期盈收结果简报会上,人们对与美国共享办公空间公司(WeWork)的合作带来的亏损表示震惊不已。

软银集团报告显示集团净亏损约为7 000亿日元,这是有史以来企业单季度亏损最严重的一次。而"罪魁祸首"就是提供办公场所租赁服务的美国共享办公空间公司。亏损主要是由美国共享办公空间公司的公允价值下跌造成的,而软银愿景基金和软银集团都投资了这家公司，后者是通过其子公司进行的投资。

记者的提问也主要集中在这些问题上。

5个月前，孙正义不断强调自己的雄心壮志——在20年内将集团市值提高到200万亿日元。但是，在2019财年中期盈收结果简报会上，他的立场却发生了巨大的转变。他一遍又一遍地说："我对自己的决定感到非常后悔。"他为因自己的决定而给股东、金融机构、投资者，以及众多的分支机构带来的担忧表示道歉。他承诺会从自己的错误中吸取教训、改善管理。

孙先生到底后悔什么呢？他又从中学到了什么呢？

首先，软银集团高估了美国共享办公空间公司的价值。2019年10月，软银集团宣布会为美国共享办公空间公司制定一套金融方案，其中包括加速发行现有认股权证，其平均认购成本约为之前投资成本的1/4。

其次，软银集团对其投资的企业管理过于松懈。例如，当初美国共享办公空间公司寻求上市时，其董事会批准为公司创始人提供"超级表决权"股票，这种股票拥有高出普通股票20倍的表决权。软银集团仅在该董事会的9个席位中占据1席，因此在这个完全由创始人掌控的董事会里，软银根本无法阻止董事会的决定。在未来的发展中，软银集团打算将董事会成员扩至 10 人，其中有 5 人来自软银集团。集团还计划为其他合资公司及未来的投资制定指导方针，并仔细审查其管理体制。

当天，孙先生冷静地剖析了软银集团的错误，并解释了公司将采取的补救措施。

然而，当被问及他对美国共享办公空间公司创始人亚当·诺伊曼的看法时，他的表情显得很微妙。

"我觉得他这个人既有优点又有缺点。我可能高估了他的优点。他在积极性、进取心及艺术性等方面的表现的确非常出色。也许，我正是被他的这些优点所蒙蔽，而忽略了他的缺点。从这层意义上讲，我非常后悔当初对他的片面评价。"

在内心深处，孙正义坚信人性本善。这不是他第一次因为这个信念而吃亏。但当事情发生的时候，他会从错误中吸取教训，展望未来。

一些资深记者评论说，随着年龄的增长，孙先生可能丧失了部分洞察力。

或许是作为回应，孙先生强调软银集团将重新评估愿景基金投资的决策方法。

其中的关键因素是自由现金流。

包括 GAFA 在内的科技企业在成立初期一直处于亏损状

态。这些企业都经过了好几年时间才迎来了良好的发展势头。

但如果你能够估算出一家企业在发展几年之后能产生多少现金流,你就可以计算出它的合理现值。

换句话说,孙先生的意思是:驱使他为企业投资的动力不只是创业者的浪漫想法。

"我对自己的一些决定感到非常后悔。"孙先生反复说道。但他对愿景基金的雄心丝毫没有减弱。

他自豪地讲述了两个事实。

其一,自3个月前第一季度盈收结果简报会召开以来,软银集团的股东价值已提高了1.4万亿日元,攀升到了22.4万亿日元;股权价值则增长了2.1万亿日元。股东价值是由股权价值减去净负债后得到的,这也是孙先生最关心的管理指标。

其二,愿景基金累计投资业绩相当可观。截至2019年9月底,该基金的未实现净收益为1.3万亿日元,已实现净收益为5 000亿日元,增值总额为1.8万亿日元。

然而,它们的未实现损失为6 000亿日元。

"从数额来看,你会发现截至目前,愿景基金的盈亏比例是3∶1。"

"无论是哪种情况,(投资初创企业)都不可能获得10∶0的盈亏比例。"

"（美国共享办公空间公司的冲击）不会带来一场风暴，只会泛起一丝涟漪。"

"企业制度一切正常。企业的愿景和战略丝毫没变。我所做的决定和遵循的策略完全是为了保证企业能继续发展。"

孙正义并非假装勇敢。

他说过的一句话特别能体现他的企业家精神：我可能会后悔，但决不会退缩。

在尝试新事物的路上，失败在所难免。重要的是你能从失败中吸取教训，并在未来做出改变。这才是失败的真正价值。

为工作而狂

2019年4月，在软银集团的职业生涯演讲中，孙正义在一群年轻人面前发表讲话，而这些年轻人正打算通过他们的第一份工作去征服这个世界。

"首先，生活在这个时代，世界风云变幻，我想给你们的忠告是永远保持对某件事情的狂热。"

"狂热"——一个强而有力的词。孙先生以此开始了他的演讲。在演讲中，他谈及这群年轻听众的日常生活。

"你这一生可曾为某件事而疯狂过？也许你曾为体育、音乐、俱乐部活动或者其他事情疯狂过，但一旦你成年后有了工作，你的职业生涯就会占据你人生的大部分时间。因此，我认为最好的生活就是你可以为工作而疯狂。这就是我的信念。"

说这话时，孙先生一定是在回忆他的学生时代。就在那一刻，他站在加利福尼亚州广阔的蓝天下，看着杂志上印着的美丽的彩色电脑芯片的图片，感动得流下了泪水。他仔细地把那一页从杂志上剪了下来，然后小心翼翼地把它保存在一个文件夹里。在那一刻，他决定将自己的人生全部献给信息革命。

"那是你愿意为之献身的疯狂，那是你值得为之献身的疯狂。想一想，我为什么对这件事如此狂热？如果你能在自己年轻的时候，在仍处于这一时代的时候，就想明白这一点，那么这个决定将对你的余生至关重要。选择你想要攀登的高山，人生的一半就已经决定好了。

"对事物的热爱将决定你要爬的山。任何人，一旦决定爬山，都是奔着顶峰而去的。但这是一项极其困难的任务。如果你的目标是日本的第一高峰，那么这项任务就已经非常难了；如果你的目标是世界第一高峰，那就更是难上加难。

"你必须思考，在你临死之前能否登顶。"

孙先生告诉听众，年轻时做的决定非常重要。

"比如，想在奥运会上赢得一枚金牌，那是一件很难做到的事。为了赢得一块乒乓球金牌，你从两三岁就开始接受训练。长到 18 岁时，你突然改变主意说：你知道吗，我真的很想打网球。然而，当你 18 岁才开始打网球，想要赢得金牌几乎是不可能的。这就好比已经爬了一半的山，却半途而废，然后下山，去爬另一座山。这样做很难取得成功，这样做就等于浪费了一半的生命。"

"人的生命是有限的，"孙先生越讲越激动，"没有什么比弄清楚你喜欢什么、你一生想要追逐的究竟是什么更重要了。我很幸运，当我还是学生的时候，偶然看到那张电脑芯片的图片，并决定去攀登这座高山。即使现在，我对它的热情仍然与日俱增。我是一个非常幸福的人。"

谁知道孙先生的哪位听众会把他的话记在心上呢？

后 记

已故的桥本五郎是我的一位挚友,他是日本软银公司执行董事兼出版部门总经理。他曾经说过:"孙正义是一个拥有模拟心脏的数字人。"

年轻时,在美国留学的孙正义创办了一家公司,并取得了巨大的成功。但是后来他决定卖掉公司,返回日本。为什么呢?

当他16岁孤身前往美国时,他的母亲因担心而伤心流泪。他当时向母亲保证,学业结束后他就会返回日本。于是他信守诺言回来了。他在日本开了一家公司。

企业家孙正义有一个强烈的信念:他希望通过信息革命让人们生活得更幸福。我还保留着1987年与孙先生第一次面谈时所做的笔记,那次访谈持续了5个小时。在我采访孙先生的

32 年间，他对技术进步的信念从未动摇。

在撰写本书的过程中，我得到了许多帮助。我首先要感谢软银集团董事长兼首席执行官孙正义。30 年来他从未失信于作为采访者的我。

在最初的采访中，我有幸听到了他对创业者充满激情的建议。

"你必须一直考虑你的想法，认真思考它，不管是睡着还是醒着。你必须对它充满热情，抱着它入眠，否则你很难超越其他人。"

"如果没有情感投入，没有远大抱负，没有疯狂努力，你永远不会等到羽翼丰满、展翅翱翔的那一天。"

因为写这本书，我非常幸运能够和孙正义的弟弟孙泰藏进行交谈。他也是一位创业者，他创立了美思乐通公司，专门投资初创企业，帮助它们进行人力资源培养。他比任何人都了解孙正义先生。

他说："我的哥哥能预测行业的未来发展趋势，他会从技术参数和金融因素角度评估科技发展。在这一方面，世界上没有人比他更擅长。

"从这层意义来看，我可以毫不夸张地说他是世界上最好的风险投资家。"

他在脸书上发布的"孙正义理论"是从本质上对孙正义先生进行了分析。

我也要感谢我的岳父三田信基先生。

在研读了由日本软银公司早年出版的《袖珍计算机库》（1981年）和《程序库》（1982年）的相关文本后，他耗尽心血为这些文本中的信息编写了一个函数式程序。他为我撰写本书提供了非常珍贵的参考资料。

最后，我还要感谢《日经大领导》杂志编辑部总编辑北方雅人和副主编兼本书的编辑小野田鹤，感谢他们对我的大力支持。

井上笃夫

2019年11月

附：孙正义大事年谱

	孙正义·软银集团	社会、经济背景
1957 年	孙正义出生在佐贺县的鸟栖市，父亲是孙三宪，母亲是李玉子。在他还是个孩子的时候，就下定决心将来要成为一名企业家。做出这一决定的部分原因是受他父亲的影响，他的父亲经营过数家企业	
1964 年（7 岁）		1964 年夏季奥运会在东京举行
1973 年（16 岁）	4 月：进入福冈县久留米市九州久留米大学附属高中 夏季：作为美国语言培训项目的成员，参观加利福尼亚大学伯克利分校 秋季：于九州久留米大学附属高中辍学	《巴黎和平协约》签署，理查德·尼克松总统宣布越南战争结束。然而，在这一声明发表后，战争仍持续了两年
1974 年（17 岁）	2 月：前往美国 9 月：在结束了一所语言学校的学习后，孙正义转到了位于美国加利福尼亚州戴利城的塞拉蒙特公立高中读二年级	
1975 年（18 岁）	9 月：开始就读于圣名大学	比尔·盖茨从哈佛大学辍学，与保罗·艾伦创办微软公司
1976 年（19 岁）	制订他的"50 年人生计划"	史蒂夫·乔布斯与史蒂夫·沃兹尼亚克创办苹果公司

续表

	孙正义·软银集团	社会、经济背景
1977年 （20岁）	转到加利福尼亚大学伯克利分校文学与科学学院读三年级（主修经济学方向）	
1978年 （21岁）	在美国成立M语音系统公司后休学，暂时回到日本。将他的发明——一款配备语音功能的电子翻译机——卖给了大型电器制造商夏普公司，并签署了一份为他带来100万美元收入的合同 与玛莎米·奥诺结婚，她在加利福尼亚大学伯克利分校专攻天体物理学	
1979年 （22岁）		由于伊朗革命和各种其他因素，第二次石油危机爆发
1980年 （23岁）	从加利福尼亚大学伯克利分校毕业，返回日本	
1981年 （24岁）	3月：在福冈市成立融乐世界——一家咨询公司 9月：在东京千代田区成立日本软银公司，最初经销计算机套装软件包。出版《袖珍计算机库》	
1982年 （25岁）	开始出版月刊《哦！PC》和《哦！MZ》，是主要向读者介绍个人计算机、软件等知识的专业杂志，并开始从事出版业务	
1983年 （26岁）	因肝炎住院，开始接受重症治疗	
1984年 （27岁）	肝炎治愈出院	由史蒂夫·乔布斯领导的苹果公司开始销售第一代麦金塔计算机

续表

	孙正义·软银集团	社会、经济背景
1985年（28岁）		史蒂夫·乔布斯离开苹果公司
1986年（29岁）	正式复职为公司董事长兼首席执行官	
1989年（32岁）		柏林墙倒塌 日本从昭和时代进入平成时代
1990年（33岁）	7月：公司名称由日本软银公司变更为软银集团	日本财务省银监局发出财产相关融资总量控制通知。日本"泡沫经济"走向崩溃
1994年（37岁）	7月：在日本证券交易商协会注册成为会员	
1995年（38岁）	4月：获得美国界面集团技术活动部门的权益，该部门正在运营世界上最大的个人计算机博览会COMDEX	微软发布Windows 95
1996年（39岁）	1月：与美国雅虎公司共同投资成立雅虎日本公司（现为Z控股公司） 2月：通过软银控股公司收购美国《个人电脑周刊》杂志出版商齐夫-戴维斯出版公司，该公司提供个人计算机行业的前沿信息	史蒂夫·乔布斯重返苹果公司
1998年（41岁）	1月：软银在东京证券交易所一区上市	
1999年（42岁）	10月：转变为纯粹控股公司	
2000年（43岁）	1月：投资阿里巴巴	

续表

	孙正义·软银集团	社会、经济背景
2001年 （44岁）	9月：BB科技公司推出雅虎BB综合宽带服务	"9·11"事件爆发 互联网泡沫破灭
2003年 （46岁）	1月：合并BB科技公司和其他三家子公司，成立软银BB公司	
2004年 （47岁）	7月：收购日本电信股份有限公司股份，进入固网电信业务	
2005年 （48岁）	1月：收购福冈大尾鹰公司（现福冈软银鹰）的股份	
2006年 （49岁）	4月：通过公开投标收购总部位于英国的沃达丰集团股份有限公司的股份，并进入移动通信业务	
2008年 （51岁）	7月：软银移动公司开始出售3G（第三代移动通信技术）苹果手机	美国雷曼兄弟公司申请破产（雷曼危机）
2010年 （53岁）	7月：启动软银金融研究院	
2011年 （54岁）	4月：发表演讲为东日本大地震筹集捐款，建立基金（软银集团捐款10亿日元，孙正义本人捐款100亿日元） 6月：成立东日本大地震灾后重建基金会 7月：成立可再生能源理事会 8月：成立可再生能源研究所 10月：成立软银能源公司	发生东日本大地震
2013年 （56岁）	7月：完成对总部位于美国的斯普林特Nextel公司（现斯普林特公司）的收购	
2014年 （57岁）	6月：软银移动公司和法国阿尔德巴兰机器人公司（现软银机器人欧洲公司）宣布世界上第一款可以识别情绪的个人机器人"派博"诞生	

续表

	孙正义·软银集团	社会、经济背景
2015年 （58岁）	4月：软银移动公司、软银BB公司、软银电信公司和雅虎移动公司合并 7月：软银公司更名为软银集团，软银移动公司更名为软银公司	
2016年 （59岁）	9月：收购总部位于英国的ARM控股有限公司 12月：成立马萨森基金会	英国通过全民公投决定脱离欧盟
2017年 （60岁）	软银愿景基金宣布首次重大关闭	唐纳德·特朗普当选为第45任美国总统
2018年 （61岁）	4月：总部位于美国的斯普林特公司和美国移动达成合并的最终协议 12月：软银集团旗下主营通信业务的子公司上市	
2019年 （62岁）	2月：由丰田和软银公司组成的MONET技术合资公司开始运营	日本从平成时代进入令和时代。福冈软银鹰队连续第三次赢得日本（职业棒球）联赛

附：孙正义大事年谱　153

愿景

孙正义一生的精进哲学

孫正義：事業家の精神

英文部分

Contents

Prologue: To Accomplish Something

(Start-Up Founders, Entrepreneurs, and Business Owners)   161

Chapter 1 Living the Best Life

Seeing People Smile Makes Me Happiest	183
I Haven't Achieved Anything as an Entrepreneur, But I Do Have the Ambition	186
Thank You, Hardship	189

Chapter 2 To Be a Genius

Masayoshi Son May Die, But Justice Never	193
The Brain is a Muscle	195
Don't Do What Other People Are Doing	199
Like Ryoma	202
It's So Good, So Good. So Exciting	205
I Decided to Invent a Method for Invention	208
A Million Dollar Contract	212

Chapter

3 Training the Self

I Just Hate Not Being Number One	217
Benefactor Gratitude Day	220
Just Being Smart Is Not Enough	226
Proceed at 70% Success Rate	230
Thinking Harder When there Seems to Be No Better Answer	235

Chapter

4 Strategy and Preparation

Business Management is Managing the Yellow	239
Life is Like Super Mario	244
I'm Angry Because I Have Something I Really Want to Accomplish	249
If an Employee Thinks 1, the Business Owner Must Think 300	252
Seven-Fold, Eight-Fold Preparation	256
Hazard and Risk	259
Top-Notch-Attack-Defense-Group	262

Chapter 5　Talk the Talk, Walk the Walk

I Will Always Honor Our Promise	267
My Hair Isn't Receding. I'm Just Advancing	270
I Would Rather Be Silicon Valley	273
Free Yourself! Fly Free!	277

Chapter 6　Theory of Technological Evolution

Read the Tides	281
Looking for the Next Jack Ma	283
Sensors, Trilobites, and the Cambrian Explosion	285
Looking Forward to the Singularity	287

Chapter 7　To All Those Who Will Live with AI

Like Young Jedi Knights	290

AI Will Redefine All Industries	293
Deviations, Delayed Reactions	296
"Big Talk" Mentality	298
I Might Have Regrets, But I Won't Shrink Away	301
Be Crazy About Something!	305
Afterword	309
Chronological History (Abridged)	313

Prologue: To Accomplish Something

(Start-Up Founders, Entrepreneurs, and Business Owners)

The goal of this book is to convey to readers the mentalities and mindsets of the entrepreneur Masayoshi Son, so that they can incorporate the knowledge in their own lives.

I wrote this book with a clear audience in mind—founders and aspiring founders of start-ups. I learned a lot about Son through my over 30 years of interviews with him, and in this book, I have laid out his choicest words and actions—the ones that most reveal the core of who he is—in a loosely chronological, biographical fashion.

Through this book, I wish to answer the question that has been asked worldwide in recent years: "Who is Masayoshi Son?"

I believe that his message should be conveyed not just within Japan, but to young people and start-up founders throughout the world.

Son maintains that he is an entrepreneur. What is the difference between an entrepreneur and a start-up founder?

In the past, he gave me this definition: "Start-up founders establish things. Entrepreneurs accomplish things. Business owners solve things." Start-up founders, entrepreneurs, and business owners. While writing this book, I asked him again what the differences were between these three, and received a message from him, on October 18th 2019, in response that is aimed towards start-up founders. I would like to start off this book with the very interview in which he gave me this response.

* * *

—You once said that start-up founders establish things, entrepreneurs accomplish things, and business owners solve things. Today I'd like to ask you about these differences in more detail.

Start-up founders have to be crazy, to some extent.

Start-up founders think about things that other people don't, and come up with things that don't exist yet.

In that sense, I think the kind of people that are suited for founding start-ups are people who are a bit from the mainstream.

—There are more than a few start-up founders who have gotten themselves into trouble with their eccentric words and actions, and been chased out of their own companies. Would you say these people were a bit too crazy?

They're all crazy. They're just...different from normal people.

And there are times when this craziness doesn't last them the whole way, when it dies out before they really get to accomplish something.

—They weren't able to become entrepreneurs.

But, they served an important role as the founder.

For example, Steve Jobs, when he was young, was chased out of Apple Computers (current Apple) because of this "craziness." But then he returned, and was able to accomplish something—to a truly amazing extent. This was the moment when the crazy start-up founder became an entrepreneur. And of course it was only possible because he'd experienced some hardships, and figured out what he'd really wanted to do.

Start-up founders might sound crazy—the things they're saying don't make sense, their actions don't make sense. But in the beginning, you pretty much have to not make any sense.

— Otherwise nothing would ever get started.

I think the kind of idea that upends how people think of the world has to not make any sense. It'd be very difficult to come up with an idea like that while trying to make sense. It's like being an artist, or a rock musician.

When I say I love start-up founders, it's because of this almost artistic brilliance. They're creating something new. It's creativity. I think very highly of that, and have a lot of respect for them.

We've invested in about 90 start-ups now through the SoftBank Vision Fund (as of November 6, 2019), but these founders are all crazy, to some degree. And the ones that are able to get their start-ups to unicorn level—they are the truly determined ones, even among the already "crazy" population of founders. These are the kinds of people that are able to turn their start-ups into unicorns, with valuations of over a billion dollars.

The founders who weren't able to get to this level, who ended their journey without making it past that billion-dollar corporate value, were horses, in other words. They weren't able to grow wings. The ones that grow wings are the ones that fly, that turn into unicorns. And those are the truly incredible start-up founders.

—Whether they have wings or not.

Wings, yes, in the sense that they don't just jump—they fly through the skies. And of course, what divides them is whether or not they're able to get over a billion dollars in corporate value. That billion dollar mark is what determines whether you have "wings." Founders who couldn't get their start-ups valued at over a billion dollars may have been jumping, but they weren't flying. They were horses without wings [laughs]. The difference is whether you're a horse or a unicorn, whether you have wings or not.

There are a lot of venture CEOs out there that call themselves start-up founders, and my question to them is, "But do you have wings?" Maybe it's just a temporary jump. They haven't been able to acquire a user base in the millions, in other words.

Have a user base in the millions, and you'll get to a billion dollars in corporate value. When you get to this level—when you capture the hearts of a million users, and provide them with new value—you'll generally become a company valued at a billion dollars.

Anything less than that is not enough. Maybe you're out in front now, but you might be overtaken. Or, the company may just peter out before it gets very big. These people, to me, are wannabe founders.

They had the passion, but they didn't have the skills. Or maybe they just weren't able to get their customers to understand them as well as they needed to. They had the idea, and devoted themselves to the challenge, but in the end, weren't able to accomplish much. They weren't able to fly. These people ultimately weren't able to get to unicorn level.

Start-up founders don't imitate others—they create new things, and take on new challenges. They "start-up" business. They don't imitate, they "start." And in doing so, they create new worldviews. That's what a founder does.

But until they're able to break through that billion-dollar level, amass a million users, I don't think you can really say they've "started up" a business. They might be working very hard towards something new, but they're not really flying. They haven't reached that level where they've grown wings. At that stage, you're still a horse, just like any other horse.

I established the Vision Fund because I wanted to support the kind of businesses capable of providing value to millions of users and that are, to some extent, sustainable.

Sustainable in this sense means they have wings, and will be able to continue flying. No wings, and all you can do is jump—then fall. Jumping and "flying" that way is different from being in continuous flight. You can jump even without wings, but you only become sustainable when you grow wings and are able to continue flying, get to the million-user, billion-dollar level. It's only then that you grow wings, and become a unicorn.

The Vision Fund works to discover these unicorns, cultivate them, and provide support so they can grow even bigger and continue their flight.

Until now, there had never been an investment group that focuses solely on these kinds of unicorn companies. There are about 5,000 venture capital firms that look for and cultivate what they think will be the next big unicorn company, but these firms are investing in companies that haven't reached unicorn level yet.

It's different when you're trying to cultivate companies that have already gotten to unicorn level [like in the Vision Fund]—different even from the amount of capital needed.

—It's different by orders of magnitude.

Yes, [it's different by orders of magnitude] from the start-up investment you'd make in a horse.

The hay and carrots you give a horse are around 10 million dollars. 10 million, 20 million is enough. But unicorns, flying through the sky...they eat rainbows. They don't eat carrots—they eat rainbows. They're flying, looking for these rainbows. The cost of these rainbows is about a billion dollars per head. So if you have 100 unicorns, you need 100 billion dollars in capital.

So when I was creating the Vision Fund, I knew from the beginning that it would have to have a scale of 100 billion dollars. I knew that from the very beginning, but when I proposed it, Rajeev (Rajeev Misra, CEO of the SoftBank Vision Fund; at the time, he was Head of Strategic Finance at the SoftBank Group) and the others thought I was absolutely insane.

—Even Rajeev thought you were insane.

At first. Rajeev said in the beginning that maybe 2 billion, 30 billion would be enough, but even that seemed like too much.

At the time, there was no fund in the world that was close to that level. The largest one was maybe 500 million, 1 billion dollars. It was common knowledge in Silicon Valley, until about two years ago, that funds would be about a billion dollars at the largest.

And so when we came out with our 100 billion dollar Vision Fund, there were many others who tried to copy us, rushing to come out with larger funds. But it's impossible to come up with that amount of money all of a sudden.

These funds have 30, 40 years of history. But the top [venture capital firms], even with all that history, would have difficulty coming up with that amount of money, and of course it never even occurred to them to do so in the first place. It's because they never thought of focusing only on the unicorns.

—So it's about limiting your targets.

The targets that we want, that we pursue, are different. Just like how your mindset, your level of preparation is different when you're trying to fish a sea bream or a barracuda as opposed to a whale. The scale of capital is different. There's a difference in the targets we're aiming for, what we're trying to do. The "thing" that we're trying to accomplish, our ambitions, are different.

I believe that these unicorns are the true start-up founders, within the larger population of start-up founders.

Those who haven't reached that level are [still] aiming to become unicorns.

—What you're saying is that many start-up founders are horses that are trying to become unicorns. And that among them, only a small handful will turn into horses and accomplish something, become entrepreneurs.

Until now, venture capital firms tended to take the "broad and shallow route," investing widely in start-ups that were trying to become unicorns. But the start-ups I wanted to support are not the ones that are trying to get there, but who have already gotten there—who have fought their way into being the best in their field, who are ready to leave their competitors in the dust, who are starting to eat that rainbow. Unicorns whose wings are already growing to some degree.

—So you can see that yes, this horse can fly.

They can fly, or they're already flying. I can see their wings.

We invest only in companies where we can see their wings—see that they've started flying, becoming a unicorn.

Of course, it's [another level entirely] for these unicorns to actually "accomplish something." More specifically, for them to become listed, and for their corporate value to grow to about 30 billion to 100 billion dollars. That's a business in the real sense, and that's what makes you an entrepreneur. And I think the lower limit of that is probably around 30 billion. Once you get past the stage where you have 30 billion dollars in corporate value and over a

million users, and begin providing your services worldwide, you get to the level of business where you're really accomplishing something. Start-up founders who get to that scale while still remaining founders—they are the entrepreneurs.

In other words, you have to have a corporate value of 30 billion dollars, and be providing value to over 10 million people, and you have to be able to sustain it. That is what it takes to be an entrepreneur. In many cases, these entrepreneurs are the founders of their companies.

Then, when the business is passed down to the second generation, the third, the fourth, the fifth...there emerge people who enable business continuity and achieve results. These people are the business owners. These are people who are level-headed, who have the know-how and knowledge, and who are able to solve things confidently and thoroughly as professional business owners.

"Craziness" is not something that's required of these business owners. What's needed is a level head and of course the know-how and knowledge. They need the kind of complex skills you need to "fly blind" and deal with unforeseen circumstances, but they don't need as much of that craziness.

But unicorn start-up founders do need some level of craziness. That driving engine, that creativity. You need that to break through.

I think in that sense, Steve Jobs was incredible.

He was chased out because of his "craziness," dealt with a lot of struggle and turmoil because of that, then came back and turned Apple—which was about to go bankrupt—into the world's number one company. He had returned as an entrepreneur. And I think, of course, that he'd been able to grow in such a significant way only because he'd experienced such struggle.

—One more thing I want to ask you about is what you need to be a leader in the upcoming age. Even start-up founders have to exhibit leadership to lead large groups of people, and "fly" in the unicorn sense. There's a lot that you can't accomplish through creativity alone as well. So what do you think people need to be a leader in the age of AI?

I think AI is going to create an entirely new world of competition.

The elements that made a business successful were entirely different before and after the Industrial Revolution.

Before the Industrial Revolution, the key to becoming a great land-owner was to have a lot of land, and hire a lot of laborers. Each piece of land had its own value, and if you didn't have enough of them, you couldn't be a land-owning farmer.

—You couldn't be successful in business without owning land.

But after the Industrial Revolution, it was different. You couldn't become an entrepreneur without understanding and knowledge of the industrial sector, and knowledge about new

technologies and the know-how to use them. And you also needed another weapon in your arsenal—capital. You needed money.

And then in the Internet age, it's become so that you don't even need money—you just need the know-how and knowledge. If you have knowledge of the Internet and the know-how to use the Internet, you could become a part of GAFA[Google/Amazon/Facebook/Apple]. And so a new age arrived.

The Internet age is [in very broad terms] contained within the Information Revolution. It is an age where the Internet created an explosive amount of value. But preceding this age, like a precursor, was the age of personal computers (PCs), and before that the age of large-scale computers.

The heroes of the large-scale computer age weren't able to become the heroes of the PC age. And the heroes of the PC age weren't able to become the heroes of the Internet age.

As to whether the heroes of the Internet age will be able to become the heroes of the AI age…I believe there's a new, completely different world of competition approaching.

In order to be a hero in AI age, you first have to have an understanding of the technological elements of AI, and have the knowledge and know-how about the technology. You also need to secure access to engineers who can make use of AI.

You also need to know what you'll use the AI for.

So far, the Internet age has revolutionized two broadly defined industries.

The first is advertising. Companies created lots and lots of web pages, and the new media of the Internet crushed traditional forms of media like newspapers, magazines, TV, and radio.

The other is retail. Companies like Amazon and Alibaba revolutionized the world of retail through the Internet—more specifically through e-commerce, through which customers have instant access to information, and can buy a product with just a single click.

Mail-order shopping did exist before the Internet age in the form of electronic communication, and even before then, through mediums like newspapers, or through TV shopping. But doing this via web pages made everything more cost-effective, faster, and allowed companies to provide more information to potential customers. E-commerce, essentially, is when the Internet became the primary medium for mail-order shopping.

Advertising and retail. These two were the only specific industries that were "replaced" by the Internet. To put this into perspective, the advertising industry comprises 1% of the U.S. GDP, and the retail industry 6%—a total of 7% (estimate by the SoftBank Group based on documents by the U.S. Bureau of Economic Analysis).

In contrast, the AI age that is now arriving will disrupt all kinds of industries, not just advertising and retail. Creating new medications in the medical world using AI, or using AI in hotels and offices, in transportation. Companies like Uber or Didi, changing the way we get from place to place. And there's also the new and growing world of Fintech, where AI is set to revolutionize the fields of banking, securities, and insurance.

What I'm trying to say is that AI will disrupt far more than the world of advertising, with its 1% of GDP, or the world of retail, with its 6%. AI will be used as a new and powerful weapon in the remaining 93% of GDP, not just in the U.S., but all over the world. And in the process, it will transform all kinds of industries.

And when this happens, it won't be enough to know how to use the Internet, or know how to type on a keyboard. You have to have an understanding of each industry itself.

——I see. You not only have to understand the AI that's doing the transforming, but the industry that's being transformed by it.

For instance, in the medical field, you have to have a deep understanding of the medical industry before you're able to transform it with AI. In the medical field, in transportation, it's not as simple as setting up a website. You have to have drivers who work for you. Real, live drivers driving on real roads. And to create

medication, you have to coordinate very closely with the labs that are conducting the experiments. All hotels had to do in the Internet age was incorporate e-commerce—accepting reservations via web pages—but nowadays, OYO is trying to change how hotels are managed entirely. OYO in that sense is very deeply involved in the management of hotels themselves.

In this kind of world, you not only need the knowledge on AI-related technologies, you also need a deep understanding of each specific industry. You need the ability to manage mixed groups of employees, and have to be able to manage these employees within a more vertical business model.

So what you need are operational skills and management skills, in addition to the know-how with regards to these new technologies. You have to have the ability to manage wider groups of people—not just the humanities-based or science-based employees on their computers all day, but also the more physical, externally-oriented employees.

You might think in the AI age that everything will come down to knowledge, but that's not true. In order to be competitive, you have to have the management skills in your specific industry, and be able to use AI as a tool in that industry.

It'll require more specialization. You can't just be an expert on applying AI to everything—you have to be an expert on applying AI in a way that's suited for one specific industry. If you're trying to use AI to analyze blood and DNA for the early detection of cancer, you have to have done a lot of research in oncology, and you have to have the skills to be able to manage hospitals, doctors, and patients directly, and sell this service to them. This is something that can't just be handled by an IT company.

And so in this new age, there will once again emerge heroes in each category. When you talk about an AI company in the AI age, people immediately think you're talking about a company that develops AI technologies. They tend to think that AI companies are the companies that they hear about on the news—like so-and-so AI beat a professional at shogi①, chess, or go②.

---

① Shogi: A traditional Japanese board game similar to chess. There was an event called the "Den-osen" held in Japan from 2012-2017, wherein professional shogi players played against a computer software. Many of the professional shogi players lost to the software, and it was covered widely in the media.

② Go: It is, however, known as a more complicated and intellectual game, and it was thought to be difficult to come up with a go computer software that could beat a human being. In 2017, however, U.S.-based Google's AlphaGo beat a Chinese go player considered to be the best in the world, with the feat reported widely in the media.

But this is just using AI as a tool. It's the same as in audio and image recognition—you're just selling a tool. And there's only so much you can do as a tool store.

At the start of the Internet age as well, the companies that were glorified were those that sold the Internet as a tool.

The same thing happened when the age of oil arrived—the first to be glorified were the "tool stores" that sold the drills needed to drill the oil. But in the end, the kings of the age of oil were those that used the drills and managed to acquire the oil. And in the Internet age, the companies that ended up winning, becoming kings, were those that used the Internet as a tool to provide perpetual services. Amazon and Alibaba didn't invent the Internet itself. The companies that were able to make the best use of this tool, use it in the best possible way, and who were able to answer to the perpetual needs of the service industry, were those that grew explosively in scale.

If we're able to use AI as a tool in the same way, there will be lots of demand for it. And the companies that are able to revolutionize industries with 10 trillion, 100 trillion yen in market potential are the ones that will grow in the future, become heroes.

That's why companies known for their amazing virtual reality technologies will be hyped up at first…

—But they won't be able to continue flying.

Yes, exactly.

—They're not sustainable.

They're tool stores. Maybe they're an exciting new tool store, with all this virtual reality technology, but what good are they doing for the world? Will it help treat cancer? Will it make it so we can buy goods for cheaper? Will it boost loans?

It's hard, with virtual reality, to tie it into making things cheaper, or creating better treatments for diseases. The question is how you'll use virtual reality—what kind of services you'll use it for, what major market you want to go into. Do that and that'd be an incredible company, but if all you're doing is coming up with the technology, coming up with the tools, all you really are is a tool store.

When we first established the company, we were selling PC software. The software that sold very well in the beginning were based around programming languages. The companies that were providing programming languages like BASIC or Fortran, or development tools and environments, were very glorified. But nowadays most of these companies don't exist. They were tool stores, in other words. And it's difficult to turn a tool store into a major, sustainable business.

—You're saying the market you choose is very important in running a sustainable business. But wouldn't you say persistence is also a factor? You take action, and continue taking action. You keep driving forward, forward, without giving up. Something you said once that I love is "Burn, burn, burn it all out."

Another thing that was very striking for me was how you kept saying, "We've entered the AI age." At one point, you asked the people around you, "Does everyone actually think that? Do you really, truly believe that?" You asked question after question, and some people revealed that they were a bit unsure, still. And they regretted their thought process until then.

I think there's just a very clear difference in these areas—how willing you are to take action, continue taking action, and commit yourself no matter what to a vision.

There are a lot of people who come up with ideas. A lot of these people often brag about it, like, "I thought of it first" [laughs]. There are a lot of people who brag about having thought of an idea first, and of course it's a difficult thing, a very necessary thing, for someone to be the first to come up with an idea. Without it, we wouldn't ever see new eras.

But to be the first to think of something…It's not like the company that was the first to make TVs is number one in that area now.

In the end, all you did in these cases was just rush in and fulfill your own wishes. You weren't able to continue winning.

The reality is that you're always going to have to deal with

all kinds of crude, horrible issues. Reality is not that easy. It's not always sunny. There are rainy days, cloudy days, stormy days.

What you have to do is not give up, not lose hope, and overcome all kinds of difficulties, all kinds of storms. And that difference...It's whether or not you're able to keep going even in a storm, without making excuses for yourself—whether you're able to grit your teeth through the tough issues, and keep flying. Whether you're able to keep going without rest. What do you need to be able to do that?

I think, of course, that the answer is just passion—crazy, powerful passion. Emotional investment.

—Crazy passion, emotional investment.

You have to be crazy to keep going in a storm, without resting, maybe even risking your life.

—You said before that people need to be crazier.

Yes, you have to be crazier.

—People aren't crazy enough.

Exactly.

Normally, people would think you're not supposed to fly during a storm, that you have to rest. If you said you were going out to fish or fly during a storm, that'd sound crazy. So what everyone does is they take the safe route, and they rest.

Even though that's actually the greatest…

—Danger, yes. They lose momentum.

No, it's an opportunity.

—Oh, on the flip side.

Let's say there's a herd of 100 horses, and only one of them is trying to fly. What that one horse needs to do is to gallop like crazy while the other horses lie down to rest. Just keep galloping like crazy, and you'll grow wings along the way.

—I guess it does come down to people not being crazy enough.

Yes, yes, exactly.

You have to always be thinking about it, and thinking hard about it, whether asleep or awake. You have to be so passionate about it that you're pretty much going to sleep cradling these thoughts, or it's going to be difficult for you to get too far ahead of everyone else.

What I'm saying is that life isn't easy, and it's not going to let you accomplish anything without you working crazy hard to achieve it.

It's that difficult. It's just that difficult to grow wings and fly.

You have to want to run, run, run like crazy through storms or whatever else stands in your way, and jump over that cliff. You have to jump over that cliff, make a mad dash for the next cliff, muster up all of your energy to make that jump, leap into the air, fall, then try and try again, falling to the ground again and again...Every time going back to the same spot, sprinting again, just wanting to fly to

the top of that cliff on the other side. And as you do this, again and again running as hard and fast as you can, you eventually start to grow wings.

Without that emotional investment, that aspiration, that crazed effort, you won't get anywhere close to growing wings.

——Crazed passion is what's needed for start-up founders, who are already crazy on some level, to get wings and grow even further as entrepreneurs. They need to be more crazy, be more serious about being crazy. Thank you for this message for start-up founders, and all those aspiring to be start-up founders.

Chapter 1

Living the Best Life

Seeing People Smile Makes Me Happiest

It was April 25, 2019, and an audience of prospective employees had gathered to watch Son speak at "SoftBank Career Live." Son, 61 years old, stood on stage and spoke to this audience of young people that would take on the 21st century.

"I would not want to live my one and only life for money."

Son's reasoning for this is based in an experience he had when he was 25 years old. It was his second year since starting SOFTBANK Corp. Japan (current SoftBank Group Corp.), and he was hospitalized for hepatitis. The doctor told him he had only five years to live. This was right after starting SoftBank, and right after his second child had been born.

All he could do was cry. Alone, in the hospital, he cried, asking himself, *What am I working for? Why am I sneaking out of the hospital to go to these management meetings, and even getting yelled at by my doctor?*

For money? But when you die, you have no need for money.

Fame? Glory? But no, he didn't want that either.

His answer, when it came down to it, was "I want to make people smile. I want to see smiles on children's faces."

His feelings, which before had been hidden deep in his soul, surged forward. *I want to see my daughters' smile. That's why I want to live. I want to see my family's smiles. I want to go to work every day and see my employees' smiles. The customers' smiles. But no, not just the customers.*

"If someone is using a SoftBank Group service on the other side of the world, it doesn't matter if they know the name of our company or if they know that it was us that made it. I just want there to be people in the world who will smile and say 'thank you' just under their breath, to themselves (about something we've done as a company), even if they don't know who to thank," says Son today.

Luckily, Son made a complete recovery from his illness, and got his life back. But he still carries his feelings from that time in the very bottom of his heart.

28 years later, on March 11, 2011—the Great East Japan

Earthquake hit. Every day on the news, there was endless footage of towns being washed away in the tsunami. It exhausted everyone—physically, emotionally.

It was in the afternoon on March 12, the next day, that there was a hydrogen explosion at the Unit 1 Reactor of the Fukushima Daiichi Nuclear Power Plant. On the 22nd of the same month, Son went into Fukushima, armed with a Geiger counter, and visited an evacuation shelter. There, he was hit again and again with the same realization.

In the face of a natural disaster that killed more than 15,000 people, human beings were powerless.

Son asked himself whether the Information Revolution, which he had dedicated his life to, could have saved people in that disaster.

If it couldn't have saved them, then what was the point of the Information Revolution? Son struggled with his thoughts, and there were nights he could not sleep. There were times also where he burst into sobs in the middle of meetings, without a care for what others would think. That period, when so many people all over Japan were struggling with their perspectives on life, was a hard time for Son as well.

Eventually, however, he came to a conclusion. "Even then, we'll move forward with the Information Revolution." How had he gotten there?

"For me, it's just to make myself happy. And seeing people smile makes me happiest."

His feelings on this have grown stronger by the day.

I Haven't Achieved Anything as an Entrepreneur, But I Do Have the Ambition

"I haven't achieved anything yet as an entrepreneur. But I do have the ambition."

August 11, 2018. This was what Masayoshi Son said on his 61st birthday.

Unlikely words from one of the most well-known entrepreneur in Japan.

"I've met with major players in finance and politics."

By major player, he means major players from all over the world.

"But I admire my father the most of all. Even now, the person I admire the most is my father."

There was a clear reason for this.

"His concentration and his competitive spirit are unmatched."

His father, Mitsunori Son, was born in 1936 as a *zainichi kankokujin*, or permanent Korean ethnic resident of Japan. To help his family, who didn't have much money, he started earning money as the breadwinner immediately after graduating middle school. He helped his mother, who ran a pig farm, then found success after leaving home by peddling shochu (Japanese liquor) and other ventures. He was a powerful and energetic man, with a personality keen on enjoying life to the fullest, and that wasn't hampered at all by his less fortunate upbringing—his sons would say about him later.

He was devoted enough to his parents to build a splendid house at the age of 19. Eventually, Mistunori Son got to the point where he ran 20 pachinko parlors. Even after that, he came up with and developed a wide variety of businesses, becoming a pioneering entrepreneur. He had started from nothing, and managed to raise four sons. His second son was Masayoshi, and his fourth was Taizo Son, who is known for being the founder of a company that invests in up-and-coming start-ups. His oldest son and his third son have also run their own businesses.

"I think of myself as the 1.5th generation of this family," said Son, expressing his respect and admiration for his father. What he means is that though he is not the second generation in the sense that he inherited his father's businesses, he has inherited many incredible qualities from his father.

Mitsunori had always praised his children from the bottom of his heart. That was how he had instilled motivation in his children. At crucial moments, he would call out to his sons, "Genius Masayoshi!"

"Genius Taizo!" He's completely serious, believes it from the bottom of his heart. Even now that they are adults, he still calls them that.

"He really meant it when he praised us. Kids can tell when you're praising them as a parenting technique. My father was the best educator. He really was sincere with us."

About living as a *zainichi kankokujin* in Japan, Mitsunori said, "You have to live by the rules or they won't accept you." He has maintained his strong beliefs throughout his life.

The four Son brothers have each achieved success in their own fields. When it comes to business, however, they all say, "No one's better than my father."

Masayoshi has called his father just to hear his voice, from when he created SoftBank Group all the way to now. "When I first started the company, it was every day," said Son.

His father knows everything about Son's businesses, from his time at Unison World in Hakata Ward, Fukuoka City, to his establishing SOFTBANK Corp. Japan (current SoftBank Group Corp.) in Tokyo in the 1980s. From when the company handled PC software and manuals, to now, 40 years later in the 21st century, as AI has started becoming a reality. He is also more focused than anyone else on the future of the company, from the 10 trillion yen "SoftBank Vision Fund" to the major U.K. semiconductor design company Arm limited, which is now under the SoftBank umbrella, and SoftBank's IoT businesses, such as the humanoid robot Pepper.

His father always says to him.

"The most fun part of business is making people happy."

Said Son, "My father understands me the best, and is my greatest supporter."

Every time Son hears his father's voice, his conviction grows stronger.

"I want to be useful to people as an entrepreneur, and work to bring happiness to the world."

This is what his father has taught him, through experience.

SoftBank broke 1 trillion yen in its consolidated annual net profit in FY 2016.

And yet Son would probably say the same thing.

"I haven't achieved anything yet as an entrepreneur. But I do have the ambition."

Thank You, Hardship

It was April 2019, and Son was speaking in front of an audience of 429 new SoftBank employees. The Japanese telecom company SoftBank has now become the core company in the SoftBank Group.

"It doesn't matter how awful or hard things are—if you have the drive, the motivation, and you work as hard as you can, you'll be able to get through it. There will always come a time when you have to face something difficult at work. You can get discouraged, or you can learn from the experience and become even better and stronger. That's up to you and your mindset. It all comes down to you. Hardships will make you a stronger person. So when I was young, I'd be happy to face hardships—in fact, I'd say thank you."

When Son said this, he may have had the following words in mind, spoken by the military commander Yamanaka Shikanosuke[1], as a prayer to the moon. "May I be given seven troubles and agonies." Yamanaka, who had attained the respect of even Oda Nobunaga[2], became a better, stronger military commander by facing up to many hardships.

Son himself has been faced with trouble after trouble, including his struggle with illness right after he established SoftBank.

---

[1] Yamanaka Shikanosuke: A military commander who lived in the same era as Oda Nobunaga, known for his bravery.

[2] Oda Nobunaga: A military commander who aimed to unify the nation during the Sengoku Period in the 16th century, when Japan was fractured into many different countries, all vying for control of Japan. Known for his innovative strategies, including the implementation of firearms from the West into battle before any of his rivals, and the promotion of commerce. One of Son's greatest role models.

One of the greatest hardships he ever faced was in 2004, when SoftBank BB[1] (former company name) suffered a leak of about 4.51 million customers' personal information. When the perpetrators, who were connected to business partners of SoftBank sales subsidiaries, were arrested for attempted extortion. Even Son understood that this incident would threaten the very existence of his company.

On January 19, 2004, Son picked up the receiver, and called the police himself.

"My name is Son, from SoftBank."

This was three days after he had received the report from his staff member, Ken Miyauchi. After returning from an international business trip, Son immediately set up an investigate committee, and worked tirelessly through the problem for three days, taking definitive action against the issue.

"I'll solve this. It's my responsibility."

At the press conference, held in February 27 of the same year, what tormented Son the most was not the almost two and a half hour Q&A session.

"Because of my belief that human beings are inherently good, we

---

[1] Currently consolidated into the Japanese telecommunications company SoftBank.

did not keep strict enough management."

As he said these words of reflection, he bowed in apology, again and again.

From now on, he promised, they would operate on the belief that human beings were inherently evil, and manage accordingly. He promised it, and put it into action.

The decision, however, to swerve from believing in the good of people to believing the bad, seemed extremely taxing on Son. That day, for him, must have been one of the most difficult and painful of his life.

Years later, in April 2019, Son stood in front of the new SoftBank employees and said, as if he were speaking to each and every one of them.

"Every person has some things they cannot and should not change, and some things they will have to change. For instance, you should always treasure human nature and passion—maintain your own identity, take care of your soul, and respect and love other people. But at the same time, you have to keep learning and evolving every day when it comes to skills and knowledge. You can't be satisfied with the level you are now."

Entrepreneurs by nature must always be learning and evolving. As you work to make things better, day by day, all while keeping that fresh spirit you had at the start, you will face many, many hardships. And these hardships will make you stronger. Which is why Son says,

"Thank you, hardship."

Chapter 2

To Be a Genius

Masayoshi Son May Die, But Justice Never

"I was born with a sense of conviction."

Masayoshi Son was born in Tosu City, Saga Prefecture on August 11, 1957, to his father Son Mitsunori and mother Lee Tamako, as the second oldest of four sons. The area where they lived was populated by ethnic Koreans, who had built barracks and started living there before the war. Son was a third-generation *zainichi kankokujin* (Korean permanent resident of Japan).

The Son family is said to have moved from China to Korea. The family was a distinguished one that had produced generals, academics, and more, and even had a genealogical record.

The Son family moved from Daegu, Korea to the Kyushu area during Masayoshi's grandfather's generation.

Masayoshi's father Mitsunori started in the fish and pork industries, then moved onto selling shochu (Japanese liquor), and finally pachinko stores, restaurants, and real estate, establishing a financial foundation for the family.

The family was poor, however, when Masayoshi was born.

"Thanks for giving me a good name, dad. You really, really gave me a good name," said Son to his father, many times.

Once, when his father dealt with him in a rather lukewarm way, Masayoshi went in and criticized his father.

"What are you doing, dad? What is this? Masayoshi was always like that, even when he was little. From around the time when he was in elementary school, he was like that—scary. In times like this he was always right, and it was scary," said his father, looking back.

There was a time when he was little when he was discriminated against, made fun of for his origins.

"Hey, Korean!" They threw a rock that hit the back of his head, spattering bright red blood.

"I wanted to die. It felt so horrible. Even now, sometimes, on rainy days, I feel the pain of this moment."

The pain remains as a scar on his soul.

But Masayoshi didn't bear them a grudge.

"You shouldn't hold grudges against people," his grandmother had taught him.

At the age of 19, Masayoshi wrote a clear and detailed life plan for himself—his "50-Year Life Plan."

In his 20s, he would make his name known.

In his 30s, he would save up capital.

In his 40s, he would throw everything he had at his goal.

In his 50s, he would "complete" his business.

In his 60s, he would pass his business down to the next generation.

"I have never once changed this plan."

"Masayoshi Son may die, but justice never."[①]

The Brain is a Muscle

"A very talkative storyteller who weaves amazing narratives," said Masayoshi Son's younger brother, Taizo, about his father, Mitsunori.

"He has so many incredible, crazy stories."

Many of Mitsunori's stories revolve around heroic deeds, and

[①] Spoken in reference to the phrase, "Itagaki may die, but liberty never!" It is said to have been shouted in 1882 by Taisuke Itagaki, a leading civil rights advocate and head of Japan's Freedom Party, when he was attacked by a thug. This phrase by Son is particularly witty in the original Japanese, since the Kanji characters for "Masayoshi" are exactly the same as the word for "justice," seigi, in Japanese—meaning the phrase can also be read, "Masayoshi Son may die, but justice never."

often follow a similar pattern: "He goes and sticks his head into things without being asked. He always goes out looking for problems, and solves them somehow. Like Ikkyu-san① in the folk tale."

There was one time, for example, when a cow pulling a cart fell into a ditch on the side of the road. The cow was stuck on its side and mooing loudly, and a crowd had formed around it. People tried to push the cow up, but it wouldn't budge. Mitsunori, who had been passing by, tried to push the cow as well—to no avail. He thought about it for a bit, and came up with a brilliant idea. He took the shochu (Japanese liquor) he had been peddling and held it up to the cow's mouth, pouring the drink down its throat. Then, he took an iron plate, or maybe it was a stick, that was lying around nearby, heated it up until it sizzled, then pressed it hard onto the now drunk cow's bottom. The cow roared and jumped up out of the ditch, and the matter was settled.

In this story, relayed through another storyteller—Taizo—you can feel the atmosphere of the village where the Son household lived, collecting their leftovers to feed the livestock. Mitsunori just has that kind of energy, a fighting spirit.

Mitsunori opened a *Yamagoya* (a mountain cabin) style café when

---

① Ikkyu-san: The main character in a folk tale modeled off the the 15th century Zen monk Ikkyu Sojun, who used his wit to solve difcult problems posed to him by shoguns. In Japan, a famous 1970s–80s anime called "Ikkyu-san" depicted the childhood of Ikkyu Sojun.

his second oldest son, Masayoshi, was in elementary school.

"There was a shanty on the road that my father took to go to work," Taizo said. "A crudely built shanty. But it had a 'For Rent' sign on it. My father's the kind of person who's always looking around for property, so when he sees a 'For Rent' sign, he can't help but be interested. And in this case, the property was on his daily commute."

It was just an old shanty in a bad location. Surely it would be impossible to do business in a place like this. But still he noticed it there every day—still up for rent, still up for rent.

Days passed, and then a whole year, and there didn't seem to be any renters.

One day, a year and a half later, Mitsunori passed by the shanty and found an old woman cleaning it.

"Are you the owner?" Mitsunori asked.

"Yes," she said, complaining, "No one will rent this place. I don't know what to do. We used to be farmers, but now we're old, and our income is not enough. If there was a renter we'd get rent, and it would really help us out."

Mitsunori said, "I'll do it—I'll rent it."

What should I do with it? He asked himself, after he'd already rented the place.

It was an old shanty, so might as well turn it into a mountain cabin-style café, he thought. To save on set-up costs, the entire family went up to the mountains to collect rocks and wood, and turned the shanty into a mountain cabin.

"Genius Masayoshi," said Mitsunori to Masayoshi, who at the time was in elementary school. That was his nickname for Masayoshi, and he used it in earnest. He spoke to Masayoshi as if he were a business partner.

"Masayoshi, what do you think? How do you think we could turn this into a successful store?"

Masayoshi replied, "Giveaways. Hand out free coffee tickets and get the customers to come."

His father used his idea. Masayoshi, who was good at drawing, drew the illustration on the free coffee tickets. The store did very well.

And so time passed in the Son household. Their father, who was always sticking his head into things, trying to get things done, paved the way for the family alongside his business partners—his "genius" sons.

In 2001, Masayoshi—now all grown up—started up the Internet service Yahoo! BB. In order to boost business for this new service, the company made the dramatic decisions to hand the ADSL models out for free. The idea reflected his father Mitsunori's influence.

"Think until your brain explodes."

This is something that Son inherited from his father and says all the time.

Says Son, "There is no limit to the number of ideas you can have. There are no limits on ideas. You have to always be thinking of ideas. How are you going to use this one mind that you have, this one brain, as effectively as possible?"

"There's always a way. The more you say 'This is just the way it is,' or 'This is too hard,' the farther away you'll get from a solution."

"The brain is a muscle!"

Son's habit of working his brain like a muscle, with the commitment of an athlete, was instilled in him by his father, with his thrilling stories.

Don't Do What Other People Are Doing

One day, when Taizo Son was a boy, he came home from elementary school to find his father, Mitsunori, at home.

"You're home," Mitsunori said, then asked his son, "What did you learn at school today?"

"Today I learned how to divide fractions. You flip it upside down and multiply them."

"I see." Mitsunori nodded, then said purposefully.

"Don't listen to what the teachers tell you at school."

Taizo was stunned. "What?! Shouldn't I listen to what my teachers tell me? Why would you say that?" He was in turmoil. Mitsunori, however, was adamant. "The teachers at school, they lie. Don't believe them."

The true meaning of his father's words only became apparent to Taizo after he himself became a father. What his father had wanted to convey was the importance of thinking for yourself—the act of critical thinking.

"Don't listen to what the teachers tell you," and "The teachers at school, they lie." For a long time, Taizo had almost forgotten these words. But one day, right around when he first became a father, it suddenly came back to him.

"My father's amazing at coming up with catchphrases."

Taizo said. His older brother Masayoshi is also good at coming up with catchphrases, something he probably gets from his father.

Another thing Mitsunori often said to his sons was, "Don't do what other people are doing."

Once, for example, his father asked him a question: What would you do if someone came to you, saying they wanted to quit their corporate job and open a ramen store? You ask them if they know how to make ramen, and they tell you no. They've never made ramen before, but they love ramen so much, and their corporate job is so tedious—they just want to try it out. If they asked for your advice, what would you tell them?

Taizo's answer: "Well, what about going to train at an established place, and learning there?" He figured it was rational advice, and probably on the mark. The aspiring ramen chef could learn the basics there, then add an original twist to his ramen, and set up his own shop. It seemed like a realistic plan. The correct answer in the Son household, however, was completely different:

"Start stewing those pork bones right now!"

Of course, the broth at that point—without any cooking training—would probably be awful. But if they did it again and again, just stewing and stewing those pork bones, tasting it again and again, putting in some salt and trying all kinds of things, at some point the result would be something original.

But to follow this path, you can't just be a little bit better than the store the ramen shop that did things "properly," going into an established store to train, and learning all there is to know. If you're only a little bit better, customers would just go to the established business.

That's why the conclusion in the Son household is, "Don't do what other people are doing."

Taizo's older brother, Masayoshi, says, "You can't outdo other people by doing the same things they're doing."

These kinds of conversations are a mainstay of the Son household.

Like Ryoma

Son is a huge admirer of the life of Sakamoto Ryoma[1]. Ryoma was a remarkable man who dedicated his life to the Meiji Restoration, and contributed greatly to Japan's evolution in the 19th century.

Son has a life-sized photograph of Sakamoto Ryoma right in front of the meeting table in his CEO's office, where he can see it 24/7.

"You're still small. It's not good enough," Son imagines Ryoma saying. Every day, Ryoma drives him to work harder.

Son read Ryotaro Shiba's *Ryoma Goes His Way* when he was 15 years old, and it changed his perspective on life.

Son saw himself in Ryoma's life.

Ryoma grew up in a family of merchants, and started from the position of a lower-class samurai. He had been timid as a child and had often been teased by children in the neighborhood. Son was also the son of a merchant and had spent time in his childhood grappling with his origins, which strengthened his sense of kinship with Ryoma.

---

[1] Sakamoto Ryoma (1835-1867): An influential samurai who worked toward the political transition from the Edo Shogunate to the Meiji government. Ryoma also established the Kameyama Shachu, Japan's first trading company (the predecessor to the Kaientai). Assassinated at 32 years old. Ryoma's life was chronicled in the historical novel, *Ryoma Goes His Way* by renowned Japanese author Ryotaro Shiba (1923-1996).

Soon after, in the ambitious spirit of Ryoma, Son "dropped out of high school in the same way you might become a lordless samurai, and moved to the U.S. at 16 years old."

Ryoma is associated with Japan's first trade association, the *Kameyama Shachu*, which evolved into the *Kaientai*. Ryoma served as leader of the revolution that led to the Meiji Restoration, but would never have participated in the new government had he lived to see its establishment.

"Instead of being a member of the Japanese government, Ryoma wanted to serve the Kaientai on a global scale. He had far greater ambitions, and wanted to interact with people from all over the world, engage in reform, and shape Japan's future."

Son aims to follow in the Kaientai's footsteps, following his ambition and turning SoftBank into a global company. He reaffirms this goal all the time.

There are times when Son comes across a difficult issue and thinks to himself, *What would Ryoma do?*

This is why he says, "I feel panic at the thought that I haven't accomplished anything, at this age. There are a lot of things I'm still very dissatisfied with about myself."

Whenever Son holds meetings in his CEO's office, there is always a replica of a wooden sword by his side.

Whenever he feels excited or agitated, he very deliberately picks up the wooden sword, then swings it down forcefully.

"Whoa!" say the executives and employees, stunned.

Son trained at his local Hokushin Ittoryu-style dojo in middle school, and his swordsmanship is not just for show. Ryoma had also been of the Hokushin Ittoryu style. This information, which he learned from Ryotaro Shiba's book, only made him admire Ryoma more, says Son.

"I think the greatest joy for me would be to close my eyes at the end of my life, and be able to think, *what a thrilling life that was*."

If you had to use one word to describe Ryoma and his life, it would definitely be "thrilling." Son has many ideas on how to live a thrilling life.

Set great ambitions. Endure hardships. There will be times where things go well, but also times where things go poorly. Work as hard as you can—do your best and leave the rest to God. Do not lie, and always honor your promises. Ask yourself if you are lying to yourself and live a true and honest life. This is how you must live.

To close your eyes at the end of your life and be able to think, "What a thrilling life that was." For that one moment, Son will work hard his entire life.

"Like Ryoma, I want to live a thrilling life."

It's So Good, So Good. So Exciting

Short stature, an Asian, somewhat childish-looking face, friendly and full of charm.

It was November 2000, and Son was in Las Vegas.

This was during the dot com bubble, and I was sitting in my room at the MGM Grand Hotel, waiting for Son's secretary to contact me. The first email arrived in my inbox. We emailed back and forth a few times, and then finally, I got word: "Son is leaving the meeting room."

Son came walking down the wide hallway of a large Las Vegas hotel, alongside several employees. Surrounded by tall, well-built foreigners, Son looked almost like a child that had wandered into the group. It was a strange sight.

But as I watched Son, walking confidently with these large men—who all worked for him—I thought, "What a cool guy."

Soon after, like a scene in a movie, the employees slipped away and Son and I began walking together.

Son was the first to speak.

"It's so good, so good. So exciting. I tremble with excitement whenever I'm in the U.S."

When Son was 16 years old, he decided to quit school and study abroad in the U.S. This was despite being enrolled in Kurume

University Senior High School, a famous school in the Kyushu area. He made the decision after summer vacation. His decision was based on his experience studying abroad for four weeks to learn English, and the sights he saw there—the boundless blue skies and vast sceneries of California.

"How vast, how blue."

Before that point, Son was worried about his future. As a *zainichi kankokujin* (Korean permanent resident of Japan), he knew there wouldn't be much of a future for him if he just graduated from Japanese high school and went to a Japanese university. All these worries, however, immediately blew away with the sight of that Californian sky.

Son enrolled in Serramonte High School in Daly City, which was south of San Francisco. He ended up skipping a grade, and after passing the high school proficiency exam, withdrew from the high school after only three weeks, enrolling in Holy Names University. He studied like a madman.

His time as what he called a "study demon" was intense. First, he placed a massive door sheet that he'd gotten at a furniture store on top of two steel cabinets, creating an enormous study desk. He laid his textbooks, study guides, and dictionaries all out on the table, unwilling to waste even a second walking to his bookshelf. He also altered his pants pockets, sewing on giant pockets where he could store dozens of pens, his ruler, and even his calculator—efficient, since he could grab them whenever he wanted. On his back was an enormous backpack filled with textbooks. Even as he ate, he would have one eye fixed on his study guides and notebooks. "One day, I want to look at my meal with both eyes while I eat," he thought quietly to himself.

And so he was able to transfer to the highly-selective University of California, Berkeley (UC Berkeley).

Son often asks, "Is there anyone here who studied as much as I did? If you think you did, then raise your hand." He's joking when he says this, laughing, but it's probably true.

One day in his school days in US, Son picked up a magazine while waiting in line at the supermarket. A wave of inspiration washed over him, so immense it was almost paralyzing.

"How unbelievably beautiful."

The tears "flowed like someone had turned on a faucet," said Son, looking back on that moment.

He was looking at the science magazine, and on it, a color print of the i8080 computer chip, with its delicate and beautiful geometric pattern. He cut the page out from the magazine, put it in a file folder, and never went anywhere without it.

"Even now, I still remember how inspired I was. That powerful wave of inspiration shaped the way I live my life."

"To work is to savor this inspiration. And what I want to do is to share this inspiration. Isn't that the happiest thing you can do?"

It was the same feeling as "that excitement I felt when I was exploring the mountains with my friends," he said.

"I'm still right in the bloom of my youth!" said Son, now over 60 years old.

"That sense of inspiration I feel when I challenge myself to new things. That feeling has stayed exactly the same for me."

The inspiration that wells up from such an unconstrained, honest persona is a powerful force—one that drives others to take action.

I Decided to Invent a Method for Invention

Alan Kay, the "father of personal computers," once said, "The best way to predict the future is to invent it."

Son, who had just transferred into UC Berkeley, was an inventor.

Son had very good grades. He received straight-As and was in the top 5% of his class in mathematics, physics, computer science, and economics. There were many subjects where he came in first in his class.

Son knew his duty was to his studies, and had decided not to take up any part-time jobs. At the same time, however, he didn't think he should rely entirely on his allowance for his day-to-day life.

He gave himself about five minutes a day to do non-study related things.

And he thought about whether there was work that could earn him over a million yen a month on just five minutes a day.

His friends laughed at him. "Are you an idiot?"

The work that 20-year old Son eventually came up with was to invent. Every day, he would invent one thing.

He would prepare a notebook, which he called the "idea bank," and then set his alarm for five minutes. During the five minutes until the alarm went off, he would concentrate intensely. If he couldn't come up with an idea in five minutes, he would give up for the day.

The ideas he came up with in those five minutes were various. For example, a Styrofoam cover for toilet seats, a tool to grab pizza so you could eat it without getting your hands dirty, and a stoplight for color-impaired people.

Over time, he began to run out of ideas. There were more and more days where he couldn't think of single thing. Now what?

"I decided to invent a method for invention."

After much trial and error, Son observed that there are three patterns when it came to inventions.

The first is the problem-solving approach. Necessity is the mother of invention. You come across a problem, and work towards a solution.

One of Son's favorite ideas, the toilet seat cover, was his way of solving all the discomfort and anxieties that surrounded the use of toilet seats, such as temperature and hygiene. The pizza tool took the same approach by solving the problem of greasy hands.

The second kind of approach involved lateral thinking—changing the components elements and properties of existing things. Revolutionary thinking. Changing color, shape, or size. Making black things white, square things round, large things small.

The stoplight for color-impaired people was born from this approach. He had asked himself what would happen if stoplight signals were conveyed not via colors, like red, green, or yellow, but via shapes such as a circle, triangle, and a square.

The third approach was the combination approach forged by joining two different things. Simple examples of this approach include attaching an eraser to a pencil, or combining a cassette player with a radio to create a radio-cassette player.

Most of Son's ideas came from this third approach.

"That approach had the greatest potential. That was my conclusion from doing this for a year."

He then created a structured system for this approach.

First, he prepared the various "parts" that he could combine. "Orange," "nail," "computer memory card." He thought of as many things he could think of, and wrote them down on cards. He started with about 300.

He then assigned each part various index numbers—its cost, novelty factors, how much knowledge he had about the item, how likely it was that it would lead to an invention, etc. There were about 40 of these indices, with varying levels of maximum points (5 points, 10 points, 30 points, etc.) according to their level of importance. The total index number was calculated by adding and subtracting the item's score on each of these indices.

Then, he would randomly pick up three parts, and combine them together. At the same time, he would also multiply the total index number of the parts. Combinations with greater results were considered more promising as inventions.

The number of combinations was roughly $300 \times 299 \times 298/3 = 8.91$ million.

He started off using cards, but later decided to use the computer for the same task.

He was able to create a list that would reorder the parts from the highest-scoring to the lowest, marking the particularly high-scoring parts with stars. All he needed to do was input the information into the database, and he could come up with all sorts of crucial insights with just a tap of the keys. If he started from there, he could definitely come up with one invention a day, on just five minutes a day.

His "idea bank" had moved from his notebook to his computer. When he submitted it to the university as an independent project, the professor in charge gave him an A+.

"You're the first person I've seen that's used the computer for something creative."

At this point, Son—in the words of Alan Kay—had predicted the future of computers. He was working to create the future of computers.

Computers do not rob humans of their ideas. Computers give wings to human creativity, and allow it to take flight.

Even now, Son has more than 50 patents for his various inventions—the things he needs to create the future.

A Million Dollar Contract

In his third year in UC Berkeley, Son created an electronic translator with a voice function.

His "idea bank" invention method had generated approximately 250 ideas. He narrowed them down to just one, and decided to pour all of his energies into turning it into a product. The idea Son chose was the combination of three concepts: "dictionary," "LCD display," and a "speech synthesis feature."

He drew up a blueprint. The keyboard would be attached to the

LCD display. Type a sentence on the keyboard, and the system would translate the text into nine different languages and read them out loud. It was essentially an electronic translator with a voice function.

In creating the prototype, Son's strategy was to hear from the world's top intellects.

Son had received As in mathematics, physics, and computer science.

"I knew I could do it myself, somehow, if I really wanted to."

However, "Just developing the speech synthesis feature would have taken me 10, 20 years. I only have so much time in my life. The idea may have been mine, but I had to gather some of the world's top specialists to work on the details if I wanted to make it a reality."

Son looked through his phone directory, and made call after call.

Who was the number one person in each field?

The first appointment he made was with a physics professor at the UC Berkeley Space Sciences Laboratory named Forrest Mozer, a world-class authority on speech synthesis. At the professor's recommendation, he also contacted Chuck Carlson. Carlson had been involved in the design of the hardware installed in the computer on the Apollo spacecraft.

Now, how to convince these top-level specialists to work with him?

First, he spoke passionately about what he wanted to do. "I'm going to create the world's first computer with speech synthesis," he said, with full conviction.

"I don't know if I'll succeed, but I believe if we work together we can make it happen," he said. "At the very least, we'll be working on the cutting edge of technology. It will provide very good research material for you as well, and serve as a learning experience."

The response: I see, that seems interesting, but are you really serious about this?

Son refused to back down in the face of reluctance. He proposed compensation. This compensation differed according to the individual. Professor Mozer, for instance, would receive a contingency fee based on the success of the product. Henry Heetderks, who took over hardware design after Chuck, would receive 50 dollars an hour. Hong Liu, a classmate who handled miscellaneous tasks, would be given an annual salary of 20,000 dollars, equivalent to the salary of a new university graduate.

While the direct offer of compensation might have shocked people, it made them realize very quickly that he was completely serious.

Son pressed on, "It'll be a learning experience, be good for the world, and will earn you money."

And so one by one, each of these top-level specialists began to ask, "What can I do?"

The most important part of the process was being confident and persuasive.

Later, I had the opportunity to ask Professor Mozer why he had taken on the project. The idea for the electronic translator itself had not struck the professor as particularly new.

"I liked that he was thinking of sales strategy, like miniaturizing it and selling it in kiosks."

They began creating the prototype. There were some delays in production, but eventually, it was complete. Son took six months off from school, and devoted everything he had to the project.

When the prototype was complete, he went back to Japan to find a buyer.

Most of the companies he met with didn't take him seriously.

He did sense a bit of interest, however, in his interview with a manager at Sharp Corpolation, a major Japanese manufacturer of electrical appliances. After the interview was over, Son called all kinds of people to find a patent attorney who had experience with Sharp. He visited the patent attorney's office, asked him about the value of his invention, and was told that it would qualify for a patent. He then asked who the decision-maker was at Sharp, and once he got the name, begged the attorney, "Please call this person and tell them they should meet with me." This was how Son wrangled an interview with Tadashi Sasaki, who at the time was a managing director at Sharp.

The license agreement that he made with Sharp was worth approximately 100 million yen.

Son likes to talk about this number in terms of dollars.

"A million-dollar contract."

There's a certain ring to "a million dollars." Son, still very much in his youth, felt like a million dollars.

His inventions had begun out of a sense of responsibility to his parents—the fact that he hadn't wanted to rely on his parents' allowance. And this had driven him to meet so many people, and brought him deep into the world of electronics. A world where he was so moved by the beauty of a computer chip that it brought him to tears. That was the world he had stepped foot in, and where he imagined for himself now a golden future.

Chapter 3

Training the Self

I Just Hate Not Being Number One

It was October 1987, and I was interviewing Masayoshi Son for the first time. I still remember his words very clearly.

"I just hate not being number one."

He said it, over and over again, his tone agitated.

"I want to get to the top as fast as possible. And if I can't get there, it's incredibly frustrating. Fundamentally, there's always this feeling that I have to be number one." Son went on to say that his own drive keeps him up at night.

The fact that he would get so mad at himself that he couldn't sleep at night stunned me. The force of Son's agitation seemed key to his personality.

Son went on, discussing why he had to be number one as a

businessperson. "When you're number one, you can endure over the long-term. When there's a recession, it's always the number twos and threes that go out of business first."

Six years before the interview, in March 1981, Son had established a company for market research in Zasshonokuma-machi in Fukuoka City.

The office was in a wooden two-story building with a tin roof, and the room was about the size of ten tatami mats, or 180 square feet, with no air conditioning. The air from the floor fan sent papers flying.

The company was not making money from market research. His ambitions were much higher than that. He wanted to accomplish something great and was using the company to think about what fields would be best for him to go into. He hired full-time and part-time employees just to conduct market research and prepare for setting up his actual business.

As a company, there was no profit.

"What business could be number one in Japan?"

Son had already settled on a series of requirements.

It had to be an industry that would grow in the future, that he could devote his life to for the next 50 years, that could act as the core of a corporate group. A unique business that no one else would think of, that would be number one in Japan in 10 years or less. A business that would make people happy, that would succeed globally in the latter half of the 20th century.

He narrowed the field down to 40 businesses. The market research for these 40 businesses was organized into stacks of papers, each stack more than one meter tall. Stack them all up, and the pile would have been over 40 meters tall.

Son read all the documents, wrote up tentative business plans for each business, and looked up the number-one experts in each field in Japan. Once he found them, he would call them and make an appointment. He wanted to ask them if his business plans were realistic. He didn't have much time to spare, and so he would always ask them to come to Fukuoka. He would pay for their fees, including their travel fees, and even pay them a gratuity. And he listened to their opinions.

He made a podium out of a cardboard tangerine box, stood on top of it, and delivered a rousing speech to his employees.

"Our sales will be 10 billion yen in five years, 50 billion yen in 10 years."

"Eventually we want to start counting in trillions."

At first, the two employees listened in silence. But over time they grew tired of Son's pronouncements, and both eventually quit.

In September, six months after setting up his market research company, he established SOFTBANK Corp. Japan (current SoftBank Group). It was a distribution business for PC packaged software. In 1982, the following year, the company entered the publishing business, publishing computer-related literature.

25 years after its establishment, in FY 2005, SoftBank's total sales broke one trillion yen. Son had achieved his dream of "counting in trillions."

"The landscape looks different when you become number one," said Son.

When you do business, he says, you always have to strive for the top. If not, you shouldn't be in it at all.

"If you're not number one, you can't create these giant, influential waves of change."

"Get number one shares in a lot of fields, then expand from there. This is truly the road to success."

"When you're in a field where you think you can do it, you think you can make it, you have to decide that you're going to be number one. And once you've made that decision, you have to work as hard as you can to make it true."

Son's passion for being number one has not diminished in the slightest, even today.

Benefactor Gratitude Day

"It all started when I met him," Son says. He is talking about

Tadashi Sasaki, former senior managing director of Sharp.

When Sasaki passed away on January 31, 2018, at the age of 102, Son wrote a eulogy.

"If I hadn't met him before starting the company, neither I nor SoftBank would have gotten where we are today. He was not only a benefactor to me and to the company—he was a great man, one who built the foundation for advanced electronic technologies in Japan, and a great benefactor for Japan as a whole."

His first encounter with Sasaki goes all the way back to when Son was still a student at UC Berkeley, in 1977.

Instead of working a part-time job, Son had decided to try to "find a job where I'd make over a million yen a month on just five minutes a day." And so he began coming up with inventions, eventually developing an electronic translator with a voice function. Sharp, a major Japanese electronics manufacturer, paid a million dollars to license the product. And it was Sasaki, who was Senior Managing Director at the time, who served as Son's contact at Sharp.

This was before Son had founded SoftBank, and the first time he had acquired such a significant amount of money.

After concluding his business negotiations with Sasaki in Osaka, Son returned to Berkeley, and found success with a business importing Space Invader arcade machines to the U.S. from Japan. He went on to buy out an arcade, setting up a detailed business plan and implementing daily accounting, ultimately tripling sales over the course of a month.

Son's success as a student start-up founder marked the beginning of the SoftBank Group. And it was Sasaki who had been there for him, from the very beginning.

Sasaki, who had seen the potential in Son early on, was an engineer known for his development of the pocket calculator. He was raised in Taiwan, China, and had studied in Kyoto University. After graduating, he began working for Kawanishi Machine Works, Ltd., traveling to Germany under military orders during the war in order to help develop a radar. After the war, he learned how to develop transistors and improve the performance of vacuum tubes in the U.S., under the directive of the GHQ (General Headquarters), and later began working for Sharp. His support for his juniors, however, extended beyond the scope of his company, with even Steve Jobs referring to him as a mentor.

Son and Sasaki's friendship continued. While Son was in Berkeley, Sasaki would meet with him for dinner every time he visited the U.S., about once every two or three months. Even after Son established SOFTBANK Corp. Japan (current SoftBank Group), Sasaki would call him for dinner every two or three months, every time he was in Tokyo. Sasaki's advice was always consistent, always kind and thorough, regardless of how well Son's business was doing.

Son's eulogy went on as follows.

"Mr. Sasaki's philosophy of 'co-creation' lies deep at the heart of SoftBank, even today."

Sasaki didn't believe that inventions were the product of one genius and his or her individual creativity. He believed that there was a foundation, built by our predecessors, upon which you engaged in friendly competition and rivalry, and that this was the key to great inventions. This spirit of "co-creation" has been passed down to Son.

"I would like to express my heartfelt gratitude for all of the generosity he has shown to me over the years, and extend to you my deepest condolences."

* * *

"No experience. No knowledge. All I had in the beginning was ambition."

On top of ambition, Son also had passion and a strong, unmatched intellect that drew many people to him.

There were many people who gave him a helping hand between 1981, when he first set up SOFTBANK Corp. Japan, and the following year, when the company went through tough times.

In order to remind himself of how he felt at the time, Son

established a Benefactor Gratitude Day on the weekday between national holidays in May, making it an official holiday for the company. In his mind, this day is just as important as the anniversary of the company's founding.

Look back on the company's benefactors and the extent of their support, and you can feel again the passion that drove the very early stages of the SoftBank Group.

Other key benefactors include:

- Yozo Shimizu. Son set up SOFTBANK Corp. Japan in 1981 after an enormous amount of research, and after deciding he would "create Japan's number one software distribution company." The first to believe in Son's dream was Shimizu, who at the time was a sales general manager for NAIGAI data services. He became Son's first vendor, supplying his company's software to SOFTBANK Corp. Japan booth at an electronics show in Osaka.

- Masahide Kawashima. He was a friend of Shimizu, and at the time an editorial writer at Asahi Shimbun. He helped connect Son to leaders in the worlds of politics, business, mass media, and academia.

- Akira Tanabe. In 1981, when Son was looking to start a publishing business in order to bolster the popularity of PCs, he had come up with the idea to sell the "Pocket Computer Library," a collection of pocket computer programs, at bookstores all over the country. Son, however, did not have any knowledge of the publishing industry. With Sasaki's help, he was able to meet with Tanabe, who was managing director at Tokyo Asahiya Bookstore, and ask him to get him in contact with a "publishing agency," or a distributor that specialized in bookstores. Tanabe, surprisingly, did so—becoming a benefactor of the company in the process.

- Hiromitsu Jogu. At the time, in 1981, he was the president of Joshin Denki, having set up Japan's largest PC store, "J&P" (current J&P Technoland), in Osaka. He made the dramatic decision to make SOFTBANK Corp. Japan the sole supplier of their software.

- Mutsuro Fujiwara was one of Jogu's officers, and at the time a manager of sales at Joshin Denki.

- Yuji Kudo and Hiroshi Kudo—brothers who served as president and managing director, respectively, at Hudson, which had produced a number of popular games. They agreed to provide their games exclusively to SOFTBANK Corp. Japan, in return for a 30 million yen deposit.

- Masayuki Gokitani, manager of the Kojimachi branch of The Dai-Ichi Kangyo Bank, Ltd. In 1982, when SoftBank paid Hudson the 30 million yen deposit and subsequently ran out of working capital, he did everything he could to get the company financing through collateral-free conventional loan. Sasaki putting in a good word helped too.

- Atsuyoshi Ouchi. Vice president of major electronics company NEC Corporation. Provided SOFTBANK Corp. Japan with 30 million yen, half the price of TV commercial slots, after Son decided, in 1982, to create a TV commercial—something that was rare for PC magazines.

What had drawn them to Son was Son's positive attitude toward life.

"Life is so incredibly amazing! I don't want to waste a second of it. I want to be grateful for everything," declares Son with a bright smile. This kind of tenaciousness could sway anyone. And Son, in turn, has worked to give back to the people who have helped him.

"I won't betray the people who have believed in me, and their faith in me."

He has met many people, and challenged himself to many things.

"For me, the happiest thing in the world is continuously finding new challenges. Life is marvelous when you're constantly aiming for new things. It's incredible."

Just Being Smart Is Not Enough

Kazuo Noda is a business scholar, also known for being the general editor for the first Japanese translation of Peter Drucker's *The Practice of Management* (1956, published by Jiyukokuminsha). It was 1981 when Son first visited his office in Akasaka, Tokyo. Son was 24 years old, and had just established his company.

Son left a vivid impression on Noda.

"He had a small stature, and was a nice young man with the same smile he has now."

At the time, Noda's office had the air of a management school, with young entrepreneurs visiting often to debate amongst one another. These members included two people that would later, alongside Son, be referred to as the "Three Musketeers of the Start-Up World": Hideo Sawada of HIS[①] (current Chairman & President) and Yasuyuki Nambu of Pasona Group [②] (current Representative Director).

Noda once asked them, "Do you know the difference between an aspiration and a dream?"

"Dreams are about desire, like 'I want this car,' or 'I want to own a house,' but an aspiration is a serious challenge you want to undertake towards the future. Don't be the kind of man that chases your dreams! Be the kind of person that continues to have and chase high aspirations," he said.

---

① HIS: Japanese travel agency established by Hideo Sawada in 1980 (International Tours at time of establishment). Their consolidated sales in October 2018 was 728.5 billion yen.
② Pasona Group: Major Japanese HR company established by Yasuyuki Nambu in 1976 (Temporary Center at time of establishment). Their consolidated sales in May 2019 was 326.9 billion yen.

Son etched these words deep within his mind.

"Son is a bright and influential person, but he doesn't really have an overwhelming personality, and he's not particularly elegant either. And yet, even after all the success he's had, he has always remained humble," Noda observed.

Son is always friendly and humble, no matter who he talks to, and most people who encounter him are probably left with that impression.

Noda theorizes that this, in fact, is the greatest secret behind Son's success in the cut-throat world of business.

As a business scholar who has witnessed many young people striving to be entrepreneurs, Noda has the ability to discern genuine capability.

Noda said to me, "If you were to describe Son in one word, it would be—just as his name suggests—justice."①

There is nothing about Son that is frivolous, superficial. He marches forward, aiming high.

Goro Hashimoto began working for SOFTBANK Corp. Japan (current SoftBank Group) in 1982, soon after its establishment, and worked his way up the ladder, eventually becoming the manager of the

---

① The Kanji characters for Son's first name, "正义," is exactly the same as the characters for the word "justice (seigi)" in Japanese, meaning " 正 义 " can be read as "Masayoshi" or "justice."

Publishing Business Division. Before his death, Hashimoto relayed Son's most memorable comment to him.

"Goro-chan (Hashimoto's nickname), which would you choose—a person who's just smart, or a person who's simple and honest, and always sees everything through? I would definitely choose the latter."

"Goro-chan" noted that Son's observation was inspiring and enabled him to apply himself at work.

There are of course people who left the SoftBank Group for a variety of reasons. Many of them, however, look back fondly on their time there. "I mean, it was hard [while I worked there], and [Son] yelled at me a bunch of times. But as long as we were honest and sincere, he was always understanding."

Son, at times, will repeat these words. "Just being smart is not enough. You have to dig deep and be extremely honest with yourself, or you will not grow as a person."

In August 2019, a young business owner received an email from Son that began, "*Madamada mijukumono desuga, yoroshiku onegaishimasu,*" an introduction generally used by young new employees that translates roughly to "I still have so much to learn, but I look forward to doing business with you."

There is no lie in these words.

Proceed at 70% Success Rate

Son created "Son's Art of War, Squared" in his twenties. Inspired by *The Art of War*, the classic Chinese military treatise by Sun Tzu, Son's strategy is summed up 25 *Kanji* characters on a 5 × 5 grid, with one character in each grid. This strategy is Son's life philosophy, with deep roots in his business philosophy as well.

Of this strategy, the part that most strongly reflects his originality is "顶情略七斗." A line that encompasses his vision.

The Kanji character "顶" (cho) means summit, and in this case means goal, or destination—vision, in other words.

"You decide the mountain you're going to climb, and that alone determines half of your life, half of your victory. Vision is extremely important."

"You have to make clear where you want to go, what your vision is. I want things to be like this in 10 years, 30 years. You have to have concrete time limits, and have a vivid vision of what things will look like when you get there."

"情" (jyo) means information—specifically, the collection and analysis of information.

"You gather information, then set your vision. Once your vision is decided, you collect and analyze information very carefully and thoroughly, so you can see whether your vision is correct."

This applies to new businesses as well as investments. For every single business move he makes, Son goes through a thorough check and analysis of the information available to him.

"略" (ryaku) means strategy.

"Strategy is what's left after you've thought everything through as much as you can and only have the essentials."

And then "七" (shichi) which is the number seven in Japanese.

"Seven is a key number," said Son.

"If this were nine, or 90%, it wouldn't work as well. When you wait around preparing until you have a 90% success rate, it's often too late. Your enemies are preparing too. To make sure you don't fall behind, you have to go for it sooner, a little sooner than the others."

But this doesn't mean sooner is always better.

"Charge in when you're still at a 50%-60% success rate, and it's very risky, an all-or-nothing situation."

And so Son's strategy was born.

"That's why it's good to proceed when you have a 70% success rate."

The number seven also implies a message about the number three—which is how Son quantifies the courage to retreat.

"That 70% has to be a very, very determined 70%—a 70% you

get to after you've thought everything through," says Son.

His strategy says that you shouldn't go into a venture that has more than 30% risk. At this level of risk, you can run away when you fail, and not lose everything. "A lizard can lose about 30% of its tail and it'll grow back. But if a lizard loses half of its tail, its organs are damaged and it dies. It's the same concept," explains Son.

He also says it takes ten times more courage to retreat than it does to fight.

Think about how dangerous a car without brakes would be, or a car that isn't able to back up.

"People who grab stubbornly onto things and can't retreat should not be leaders!"

Son also said, "When the time goes, run away as fast as you can, without fear of embarrassing yourself or what other people might think. Just retreat! You shouldn't continue a fight just because you are too stubborn to leave."

Son's reputation is that of a risk-taker, who takes on incredible challenges and who seems to prefer adventure and gambles in his business decisions. Indeed, the concluding character in his five-character vision is "斗"(to), or fighting spirit. It doesn't matter how lofty your ideals, how much information you collect, how thorough of a strategy you come up with, or even whether you're 70% certain of success—you cannot accomplish anything without fighting for it. And so Son will fight for his vision, with everything he has.

The truth, however, is that he is extremely cautious.

Son's younger brother Taizo Son, an entrepreneur and investor, explains his brother's behavioral principles with an apt analogy.

"My brother is a very cautious person. There's a Japanese saying about those who are overly cautious: 'People who knock on stone bridges before crossing them.' My brother will knock on a stone bridge many, many times. He won't cross most of them, but once he does decide to cross one, he'll cross it with a dump truck."

In the words of Masayoshi Son...

"Those who stay stubborn are idiots."

"Those who cannot retreat are idiots."

"Those who cannot retreat are stingy."

He said, smiling.

"I try all kinds of things, but I make sure that the core of my businesses protected even if I have to retreat in other areas. Then I can always come back and try again."

"Although that may be why people think I never learn."

Son's eyes when he said this were not smiling.

They told the story of what a person can achieve when they are not afraid of retreat.

道	天	地	将	法
顶	情	略	七	斗
一	流	攻	守	群
智	信	仁	勇	严
风	林	火	山	海

Son's Art of War, Squared

Son's vision as expressed in 25 Kanji characters, some by Sun Tzu and some by Son himself.

The gray squares are the words of Masayoshi Son. The others are by Sun Tzu.

These 25 characters represent every element you would need to consider in making all kinds of business decisions.

The first line, "道天地将法" is what you need to win battles, as in "道," or "journey," which expresses one's philosophy.

The second line, "顶情略七斗" is the wisdom that a leader must have, as in "顶," or "summit," which expresses one's vision.

The third line, "一流攻守群," is the battle strategy for those who want to be number one, as in "一流," or "top-notch," which expresses one's dedication to being number one.

The fourth line, "智信仁勇严," expresses the knowledge and understanding one needs to be a leader.

The fifth line, "风林火山海," expresses how one must engage in battle.

Thinking Harder When there Seems to Be No Better Answer

There are two individuals who have known Son since the very beginning of the SoftBank Group.

Masahiro Inoue began working for the SoftBank Research Lab in 1987, then transferred to SoftBank (current SoftBank Group) in 1992. He was the same age as Son, with a calm, collected demeanor and a penchant for doing things in his own way. He also worked as an executive secretary at the CEO office for two years, starting from 1994.

"Son's power of concentration is just incredible. I've seen him walk into a telephone pole because he was concentrating so hard on thinking about something."

When Yahoo Japan (current Z Holdings) was established in January 1996, Inoue worked on the project as Son's closest advisor. He was appointed president in July of the same year, and worked to bring Yahoo Japan to its current state of prosperity. He stepped down from Yahoo Japan in 2012, and passed away in 2017 in a car accident. Before his death, he said the following about Son.

"I think what's amazing about him is that he has this very dynamic, big-picture side to him, as well as a narrowly-focused side that allows him to hone in on numbers and other details. Many people that have one or the other, but not many people have both."

The other individual is Ken Miyauchi (current president & CEO of SoftBank), who entered the then newly-established company in 1984, working at the very front lines of sales. Son's nickname for him is "Miyaucchan," and he is Son's ultimate right-hand man. In 2003, he said this about Son.

"I think Son's strength is his ability to 'use' people well. Meetings with him don't feel like we're just sharing information in a closed box. For example, when we want to acquire a company or settle a negotiation, there's always the question of who the right person is for the job? He always wants to get down to the very bottom of that question. He has a logical side and an emotional side, and he uses both of them very well."

Son himself has mentioned that SoftBank Group meetings are very open, sometimes to the point of discomfort and awkwardness.

"It might seem like a one-man show. But in our actual meetings, there's so much discussion and dispute, and my proposals often get rejected."

People voice their opinions freely and openly in SoftBank Group meetings, without worrying about others' positions in the company. This corporate atmosphere hasn't changed since SoftBank's founding.

Son says, "We think, think, and think, and make sure everything has been thought through. We put forward extreme financial scenarios, then work it down until everything is simplified, and a different solution might emerge.

"The right brain comes up with the 'explosions,' the ideas. The left brain makes it a reality. Having both of these makes you more persuasive, allows you to keep winning.

"Always think in terms of numbers. Always work with a logical mind.

"Being smart is important, but it comes down to whether or not you have the determination and tenacity to make things a reality. Personality-wise it's important that you don't stop, don't give up, don't get tired of the work.

"The essential quality you need to accomplish your dreams is to be totally absorbed in what you're doing."

There was one thing about Son that both Inoue and Miyauchi had admired.

"Even when there seems to be no better answer, he'll delve even deeper and think even harder."

Son will ask as many people as possible for their thoughts, then think deeply about the issue at hand before making a decision.

"He feels a powerful sense of responsibility," said Miyauchi, getting to the core of Son's strength.

This is precisely what makes Son a leader.

Chapter 4

Strategy and Preparation

Business Management is Managing the Yellow

"First of all, you don't have enough of a strategy. Do you even have a strategy?"

This was Masayoshi Son yelling at his younger brother Taizo.

It was Taizo's third year studying for the University of Tokyo, having failed the entrance exam twice. He had just started living on his own in Tokyo, when his older brother Masayoshi had called him up to meet.

Masayoshi is 15 years older than Taizo, and had even chosen his name when he was born. In the particular culture of the Kyushu area, Son, as the older brother, had total dominance.

As Taizo mumbled, "I'm inferior," "I guess it doesn't have to be the University of Tokyo," "Maybe I shouldn't even go to university," Son flew into a rage.

"It's not about whether or not you want to go to university or what university you want to go to!"

What Son wanted to know was whether his brother had "given it his all."

"You're sitting there all cynical, making excuses for yourself, refusing to look inward or face society. Are you happy like this, living such a half-hearted life?"

"No. I don't want that life."

"It's your attitude towards life that's the problem."

Taizo endured over an hour of this lecture, which he says felt like "rubbing salt into a wound."

"Don't get used to losing! Don't become a loser!"

Finally, Son began discussing strategy.

"You're probably doing your best day-to-day," Son said. "But that's not enough."

"Strategy is about how you distribute your resources."

There was no guarantee that Taizo would end up passing the exam.

But there was one thing he could do for certain: Define exactly how much he would have to study to have the strongest possible shot at passing the exam. How many textbooks and reference books would he have to read to get there? How many practice tests? This was definable. So calculate it.

That was Masayoshi's order. But he must have thought it was too difficult, because he loosened the requirements.

If it was too difficult to set an amount, he said, go out and buy all the study material you can find.

"Go to the Yaesu Book Center. Buy all the study material you can find."

Masayoshi told his younger brother Taizo, who had just moved to Tokyo, that there was a large book store in Tokyo called the Yaesu Book Center, which was stocked with more books than he could imagine from the bookstores in Kurume.

Taizo called his father.

"I'm buying reference books. Please lend me 100,000 yen. I'll pay you back with interest."

He bought many cardboard boxes full of reference books, then read each reference book and answered practice questions for thirty minutes each. He calculated how many pages he could do in thirty minutes, and calculated how long it would take him to complete one book. He then assumed he had 16 hours per day to study, and had 5,760 hours until the exam, then came up with a one-year study schedule, broken down into hour-long increments.

There was one "business plan secret" he had learned from his older brother.

Prepare for discrepancies between estimates and actual performance. Create a buffer.

From 8:00 A.M. to noon would be "Session 1." During this time, he would go through a different reference book every hour. How many pages of which book he would go through was detailed in his one-year plan.

From noon to 1:00 P.M. was the buffer —a blank space on the plan. This gave him time to recover if things didn't go according to schedule in the morning.

From 1:00 P.M. to 5:00 P.M. was "Session 2." 5:00 P.M. to 6:00 P.M. was the buffer.

There are times, however, where you still can't recover properly. That was why Taizo left his Sunday mornings open. On Sunday mornings, he would do all the things he wasn't able to complete from Monday through Saturday. And if he couldn't recover properly, he left one open day at the very end of each month when he could complete all of the remaining work.

He thought of the process in terms of a dam. Even if some things slipped through the cracks, he would find a way to keep it all in. He'd have multiple dams a day. What he couldn't recover then, he'd recover in the dam at the end of the week. And what he couldn't recover there, he'd recover at the end of the month.

If everything went according to plan, he would color that part in his plan green. If he wasn't feeling well or if he didn't feel like studying, and didn't get anything done, he would color that part red. He would color it yellow if he was able to complete it partway.

A month later, Masayoshi asked to meet up again. He wanted to know how the plan was going—a mid-term report for Taizo's business plan.

There were quite a few days in the one-year plan that were colored red, meaning he hadn't gotten any work done. Taizo thought his brother would yell at him for that, but he didn't.

"What is this yellow here?"

Masayoshi ignored the red parts. But his expression was severe.

"Open that yellow page there. How much of that did you do?"

"I did half," said Taizo.

"I'm going to test you on it, right now," said Masayoshi, then began asking him English practice questions. Taizo could only answer 20%-30%.

"You said you did half, right? What is this then?"

"Um, I don't know."

"What you wrote is a lie. This is a false report. You said you did half, but you didn't do half."

Masayoshi admonished Taizo yet again. "Humans are weak beings. They always want to make themselves look better, so they say they did half when they've really only done a third."

There was no problem, Masayoshi said, with the red parts, the parts where he reported he'd done nothing.

"Red means zero, and there's no leeway there. But this yellow…"

Masayoshi's company, SoftBank (current SoftBank Group), was on a growth trajectory, and he turned to it as an example.

"SoftBank has 3,000 people right now. If 3,000 employees said they did half of something when they only did a third, how much of a discrepancy would that produce between estimates and actual performance? Managing the yellow right here is what business management is about."

Taizo was convinced. He got the second highest score in the country on the University of Tokyo mock exam, then passed the entrance exam for the university. While at school, he set up his own company. Taizo became a business owner, and the lessons he learned from his older brother resonate to this day.

Life is Like Super Mario

In the year 2000, the dot-com bubble burst.

Taizo Son was 28 years old at the time, and was the president of a web design and system development company, overseeing about 80 employees. Suddenly, all the work he had lined up for the next month onward disappeared, and he was at a loss as to what to do. How would he pay his employees? He had little experience as a business owner. He didn't have the skill to negotiate with banks, or even a network of people he could turn to.

"My only option is to die and apologize to my employees that way."

Mentally, he was almost at his limit.

It was around this time that his older brother Masayoshi Son invited him to dinner.

His brother, as always, spoke with passion about the bright future of the Internet. Taizo, however, was in low spirits. He couldn't bring himself to say the words that he'd wanted to say for a while now, the words that were caught in his throat—that he needed to borrow some money.

As they were leaving, Taizo was finally working up the courage to ask the question. That is, until his brother touched on it first.

"Hey, I'm not lending you any money."

"Uh, I didn't..." said Taizo, stunned.

"It's written all over your face. I'm not lending you any money."

With these words from his brother, Taizo began to laugh.

Like their father, Mitsunori, Masayoshi was good at reading people, and approached them straight-forwardly, directly.

"How much?" Masayoshi asked.

Taizo's answer was straight-forward as well. "15 million yen. I've tried everything."

Masayoshi said, "15 million yen for you is a huge amount of money. The truth is, I'm struggling to figure things out too. I'm struggling to figure out where to find 15 billion yen."

He continued, getting to the heart of the matter.

"15 million yen—it wouldn't be impossible for me to lend you that money. But it wouldn't be good for you."

He explained his reasoning using the strategy for a video game.

"You haven't even cleared a single level in Super Mario. You're being killed by the weakest enemies, the Koopa Troopas of the game. You can't even get on the clouds."

He went on, saying he himself had cleared about 15, 20 levels. "It's very hard," he said.

It would be easy for him to teach Taizo how to use the green pipes to warp to level 3. "But think about it—the kind of person who'd get killed by those Koopa Troopas turtles would die instantly in level 3, even if they were to warp there. You'd die in a second."

Masayoshi then went on his final offensive.

"Just be killed by everything! Be killed by everything."

What he meant was this: "It's not okay to clear these levels randomly. Chance, luck—that's not okay. You have to get yourself caught in all of the traps and enemies in level 1, and only once you know it completely, move onto level 2. Then, be killed by everything in level 2 too, get to know the level completely, then head into level 3. If you get through a level and die, you can catch up to where you were very quickly. But if you get to level 8 by accident, because of luck or chance, and then you die, it'll be incredibly difficult to start again from level 1."

He was right. Masayoshi's powerful analogy was very persuasive.

Masayoshi said to his brother, "I could lend you the money."

"No, no," said Taizo hurriedly. "I can't borrow from you after hearing all that."

He found himself laughing. For a second, his older brother's aggressive lecturing had made him angry. Now, however, he was strangely calm. His heart felt lighter.

"Life is like Super Mario."

Like a game, Taizo thought. And if it was a game, he decided, then he'd strategize his way through it.

"What doesn't kill you makes you stronger."

After this dinner with his brother, Taizo went around visiting his clients.

There was still work to be done, like the design of websites with significantly reduced budgets. In going around to these clients, Taizo revealed the true costs of the project, and proposed that his company take on the projects at cost price. This would mean cutting their prices in half—no, to less than half. He also offered to complete the projects in advance of the original schedule. "Really? Is that alright?" The client would ask, surprised. Yes, he would say, but in exchange…

"Could we have half the payment in advance?"

It didn't matter how much their profits went down—as long as they had enough cash to go around, the company wouldn't die. One by one, Taizo's clients accepted this offer, and ordered their projects from his company.

Looking back on that time, Taizo says, "I'd made up my mind, and I went to visit them all with the commitment of a *samurai* about to commit *seppuku*. I think they felt that in me."

His brother Masayoshi's "tough love" approach had driven Taizo to complete level 1 of Super Mario, all on his own. He had overcome a tremendously difficult time.

After this, Taizo became a serial entrepreneur, eventually founding Mistletoe, a company that invests in start-ups that are committed to solving major world challenges, cultivating talent, fostering community development, and more.

He said he recently told some entrepreneurs in Ukraine about this Super Mario story, and that they had related very well to the anecdote. Ukraine is another country, alongside Estonia—which Taizo has called "the most exciting country in the world"—that is experiencing a remarkable increase in start-ups.

I'm Angry Because I Have Something I Really Want to Accomplish

"I'm angry because I have something I really want to accomplish."

On January 6, 2001, the Basic Act on the Formation of an Advanced Information and Telecommunications Network Society went into effect in Japan. The law was established in order to encourage the establishment of Internet-related infrastructure and loosen Internet-related regulations.

"The time's come. I've been waiting for this day."

It was the year after the dot-com bubble had burst. Stocks were still on a downward trend.

"We have no money. But if we don't do it now, when are we going to do it?"

It was an all-or-nothing challenge.

"I'm going to give this all I've got."

Son decided to pour the entirety of the company's resources into broadband.

At the time, dial-up Internet was the norm in Japan. The country had fallen far behind Korea, which had sped ahead with the establishment of ADSL (asymmetric digital subscriber lines), and the always-connected, broadband-style Internet.

Son's plan: to make Japan's Internet, which was ridiculed by some to be "the world's slowest and priciest," into "the world's fastest and cheapest." He prepared himself for the upcoming battle. He had one singular goal—to provide the world's best broadband Internet.

On June 29, 2001, BB Technology (current SoftBank) announced the establishment of "Yahoo! BB." The service would provide ADSL at approximately four times the speed and about a quarter of the price offered by Internet giant NTT. About 180,000 people registered for the service overnight.

But, the lines wouldn't connect. They were bombarded with complaints from customers. In some cases, customers had to wait six months before the lines connected.

The construction needed to open up the lines—construction in NTT buildings—was being heavily delayed. NTT was clearly holding back construction on purpose.

They made many requests for NTT to solve the issue, but it didn't get better. Son's anger was explosive. On June 29 of the same year, Son marched into the Ministry of Internal Affairs at the supervisory agency, his face a mask of rage.

"I am not making them wait any longer. If you don't come down on NTT, nothing will get done. I'll need to borrow a lighter."

He was serious. He was genuinely ready to give up his own life.

"I'll apologize to the customers in a press conference, tell them we can't go on with Yahoo! BB. I'll explain to them the reason why we can't provide them the service."

Soon after, the procedures for the lines began to go much more smoothly.

And two years later, in 2003, the International Telecommunication Union (ITU) recognized Japan's broadband Internet to be the "fastest and cheapest broadband" in the world. He had achieved his dream of providing "the world's fastest and cheapest" broadband Internet.

"Information Revolution—Happiness for everyone." Son is serious about accomplishing this goal.

Saigo Takamori[①], who devoted his life to building the new Japan, alongside Sakamoto Ryoma, once said, "The person who doesn't care about his own life, or reputation, or official rank, or money, is hard to control."

Son was exactly that kind of troublesome man.

"I just want people, sometime in the future, to be happy about what I've created."

---

① Saigo Takamori (1828-1877): Started as a lower-class samurai in the Satsuma Domain and built a name for himself at the end of the Edo Period, helping advance the political transition from the Edo Shogunate to the Meiji government. Eventually led a revolt under the new government, was defeated, and died by suicide. His sincerity, illustrated in novels such as Ryotaro Shiba's *Tobu Ga Gotoku*, earned him many fans amongst Japanese business owners. This quote comes from the *Nanshuoikun*, a collection of his sayings before his death.

He had accomplished this not for self-interest, but because he wanted to make Japan's Internet users happy.

Son's "anger" brought forth a revolution in Japan's Internet.

Anger, at times, can provide an immense source of energy for a revolution.

If an Employee Thinks 1, the Business owner Must Think 300

"Business owners have to consider any and every possibility."

Masayoshi went on, asking his younger brother Taizo, "Let's say, for example, that the amount of thinking an employee does for his company is '1.' In that case, how much should a business owner be thinking about the company?"

This kind of conversation happened daily in the Son household, and the question itself wasn't particularly surprising. Taizo thought to himself, "Obviously the business owner has to think about the company a lot more than an employee—probably three or five times as much, but I'm guessing, Masayoshi being Masayoshi, that the number is more than that."

So he said, "Maybe 10?"

Masayoshi was livid. "Idiot! The business owner has to work 300 times more."

Taizo was struck.

This is how Taizo learned so much about the mindset of a business owner from his brother Masayoshi.

Another example involves what to do when you absolutely need to persuade someone to do something.

Think of a minimum of 100 reasons why the person would say no to your proposal. Then, think of methods that would convince them even with all of these counterarguments, and prepare a set of questions and answers to get you there.

Masayoshi said, "You can't just quibble over details or try to forcibly convince them. The person will not say yes unless you prepare a logical argument that they truly understand, that makes perfect sense to them."

Ever since, Taizo has taken it upon himself to create a set of reasons why the other side may say no before he heads into any negotiation. Once he started putting this into practice, he realized just how one-sided his perspective had been in the past.

"It's really taught me a lot. There's a big difference between knowing something logically, and being able to truly understand and act on it."

Son is often referred to as a "jijigoroshi," a Japanese slang term that means someone who is very good at garnering the support of older men.

Even through the establishment of SOFTBANK Corp. Japan, there were many important people who bet heavily on Son's success, as if they had been bewitched by him.

Perhaps there's something about Son's natural aura that enables him to win people over. When it comes down to it, however, his skills of persuasion are the fruit of an insane, almost unbelievable level of preparation.

"If an employee thinks 1, the business owner must think 300," and the "100 possible counterarguments." Many of the lessons that Son imparted to his brother Taizo are characterized by large numbers. For instance—he should check 1,000, even 10,000 management indices, called the "1,000 knocks method" and "10,000 knocks method" (a method in which you exhaust 1,000 and 10,000 possibilities) to analyze information.

Masayoshi once said to Taizo that his thought process was similar to the "major league training brace" in the manga series *Star of the Giants* [1]. This brace was an imaginary tool used in a series that ran in the middle of Japan's high-growth postwar period in the Showa Era, and represented a spartan, rigid training method. As a child, Son had been inspired by the *Star of the Giants* series, at one point wearing iron clogs

---

[1] *Star of the Giants* : A baseball manga that was extraordinarily popular with boys in Japan in the 1960s-70s. The main character, Hyuma Hoshi, goes through very strict, intensive training under his father, and aims to become the star of the Yomiuri Giants, a famous professional baseball team. One of the most well-known examples of what is called a "supokon manga," or a sports-themed manga with an emphasis on grit and determination ("konjo").

for a while to try to strengthen his legs so he could be better at soccer.

What does Son mean, as a business owner, when he refers to this symbol of hard, spartan training?

What he means is this: It's not just about what you do, it's about how much you do it. What makes Son extraordinary is not necessarily setting the strategy itself. It is what comes afterwards—making sure that his strategy works completely, committing himself to its implementation.

When seen in hindsight, there is generally a simple causal relationship behind a successful person or endeavor. In all fields and all industries, what separates success from failure is how thoroughly you prepare, how well-built your strategy is, and how persistent you are in its implementation.

Taizo says seriously, "It's actually this part that's the hardest. It's just a piling up of mundane tasks, and of course you don't get amazing results right away, so you tend to run out of steam in the middle and give up. This may be the reason why there are so few success stories."

His older brother's lessons are unchanging. He'll change his words around but always strike at the same point, again and again. And so Taizo says, "This, I think, is the greatest secret to success."

Seven-Fold, Eight-Fold Preparation

"When you're getting into something, how much do you think you should personally prepare for unforeseen circumstances?"

Masayoshi's question was directed towards his younger brother Taizo. As always, Masayoshi's tone was chatty, casual. Taizo was caught off guard. He had never thought about anything like that before.

"Well…I mean, I do prepare alternative solutions for when things don't go properly. Are you talking about an alternative for when even the alternative doesn't work?"

Masayoshi said to Taizo, "So what you're saying is that you prepare one alternative, two at the most. That's not enough. I always have four, five alternatives lined up. And when I think even that's not enough, like for a really big gamble, I'll come up with seven or eight."

It was hard enough to come up with even one alternative, and Masayoshi was telling Taizo to have four or five prepared at all times—so that if this didn't work, he could do that, and if that didn't work, then he could do this…and so on. What's more, Masayoshi was saying that he himself was always this prepared.

Taizo confesses, "Honestly, I was taken aback. Like, how prepared could one person be?" But he explained what Masayoshi meant. "I think what my brother wanted to say was that, no matter the risk you take in your challenges, you can't let it kill you. you can't take on critical, irrecoverable damage."

"Son's Art of War, Squared," which expresses Son's strategic outlook on life, ends with the five Kanji characters, "风林火山海." "风林火山" is a story written by Sun Tzu, as well as the slogan of Japanese samurai Takeda Shingen.

The characters, "风林火山," or "wind-forest-fire-mountain," represent the premise of being "as swift as the wind, as still as the forest, as fierce as the fire, as firm as the mountain," and sums up the strategy for brave and courageous battle. To this, Son had added the character "海," or "ocean," to mean that after a victory, you should envelop the enemy and everything around them like an ocean.

Shingen's rival Uesugi Kenshin is also known for his skill and elegance in battle, but Son isn't a fan of Uesugi's principles. Son even wrote the following in a guest article in a magazine.[①]

"Uesugi Kenshin wanted to fight beautifully, looking for art and the meaning of life in battle itself. And of course, plenty of people have romanticized his battles and revel in his stories. Personally, however, I don't feel the need to earn praise and acclaim by taking on new businesses with lower success rates in order to score dramatic wins."

[①] Source: "Sun Tzu Quotes that Serve as Mottos for Leaders," PRESIDENT (January 1997)

Son's ideal battle strategy is the tried and true method—winning without having to battle, winning while expecting to win, winning by formulating a strategy so accurate that your victory is assured by the time you've gone into position.

His brother Taizo explains, "There are times, in extremely difficult situations, when the only way through requires desperate, life-or-death decisions. In such critical moments, this kind of conviction is what makes the difference between victory and defeat. There's no question that that's important. But if you're making everyone you work with make life-or-death decisions every time, if they're always in desperation mode, then you've failed as a leader."

Tadashi Yanai is the Chairman, President and CEO of FAST RETAILING, which has made Uniqlo into a global brand. Yanai listed FAST RETAILING on the market in 1994, the same year that SoftBank (current SoftBank Group) was listed. Son considers him a peer, and in fact Yanai also currently serves as an External Director for the SoftBank Group.

He had asked to meet with Son for the first time when he heard SoftBank was doing its daily accounting with computers and LAN networks, wanting to learn their methods.

Daily accounting allows businesses an understanding of various managerial indicators such as sales and profit, on a daily basis, enabling them to notice and handle unforeseen circumstances with more speed. This kind of cumulative insight is what allows for "winning while expecting to win," as opposed to sheer miraculous victories.

Not a beautiful, striking victory, but a simple, straightforward one.

This point, made by a fellow business leader, strikes at the heart of Son's approach.

Hazard and Risk

You are a RISKTAKER as much as I am.

—Bill Gates, *The Road Ahead*

So said the message that came with the book by Bill Gates of Microsoft.

Son considers this personal message from Gates to be "the greatest honor" and is very proud of it.

Son differentiates risk and danger very clearly, according to his younger brother, Taizo.

"The only kind of danger you can call 'risk' is danger you can manage, danger where you can estimate the worst possible damage. Everything else is just danger."

Thus, Masayoshi says, "You can take risks, but you can't take on danger."

Danger the way Son means it here may be closer to "hazard." Risks and hazards: You have to clearly understand the difference between the two. Gates understood that, and said Son was a true risktaker.

Son warns against the idea that make-or-break actions without the ability to estimate potential damage is heroic, amazing, or courageous.

"Maybe one time you'll get lucky and things will work out. But the success of a business is based on many, many battles, and if you keep going that way, you will fail eventually. That's why you can't take on hazards."

But the line between risks and hazards are often blurry. What do you do if you can't distinguish between the two?

Would you decide to take the action, even if it's unclear whether it's a risk or a hazard? Or would you decide not to, and choose inaction instead? What would Son do?

Son would not leave it unclear. Son would determine whether it was a risk or a hazard.

"In the case of right or wrong, he will analyze every single unknown down to the last detail," says Taizo, who has witnessed his brother do so many times.

Son will find that line, somewhere in the gradation between risk and hazard. He won't stop until he has it.

Like looking at countless yellow lights, figuring out which ones are actually red, which ones are green. Even before Son set up his first company, he paid experts to come to Fukuoka, paying their transportation fees plus gratuity, in order to draw conclusions from the massive amounts of market research he had done.

Now, he calls people from all over the world to ask questions.

If he feels the line between risk and hazard is blurry, "he'll pick up the phone right then, no matter what time it is, and just start calling people—for example, 'Hey Jack!'"

"Jack" is Jack Ma.

"I mean, Ma is probably very busy too," laughs Taizo.

"I'd like to ask you a question." That is the first thing Masayoshi says when they pick up the phone.

The kinds of people he calls during these situations are all top-tier people in their fields. That is his rule, and has been his practice. He did this even before he himself was a top-tier businessperson. Son gets the latest information from top-tier minds, and decides whether the action in question is a risk, or a hazard. He does not leave it unclear.

Son's true brilliance, however, lies in this fact—the fact that, after all this careful, deliberate analysis, he will be able to make a "maximum possible damage" estimate of a gamble that seems to everyone else like an impossible hazard. As he said, once you can make an estimate of the maximum possible damage, it ceases to be a hazard. You can take measures to prevent damage. And so the hazard turns into a risk. This is not something that any ordinary person can do, however.

"I still don't understand," Son will say, again and again, to the people around him.

His sharp and tenacious mind turns "hazard" into "risk."

Top-Notch-Attack-Defense-Group

Devote your life to a vision. And if you're going to devote your entire life to it, you better have a plan. You have to have a strategy. And what does that strategy have to be like?

Son's own answer to this question is embodied in "一流攻守群." These are five Kanji characters out of the 25 expressed in Son's Art of War, Squared.

"一."

This, the Kanji character for the number one, expresses his commitment to being number one.

"In elementary school I was almost always number one. I feel a bit sick when I'm not number one." He explains, however, that "I've never thought that I want to be number one in terms of music. I'm a lousy singer."

"But in fields where I feel like I could succeed, I decide to be number one. I absolutely need to be number one, and by a huge margin."

"You have to find a path for you to be number one, before you take a single step into that field."

"If you're number two, you've failed."

"If you're number two, you're still on your way. Finish it."

Simply being number one, however, is not Son's objective.

"Only after you become number one by a huge margin do you get to savor the true meaning of that status."

"Once you become number one, you have more space and time to think, can challenge yourself to new things. You can develop new technologies, and be more considerate of your customers. I want to be responsible in the truest sense of the word."

That's why he declares, with his broad smile, "It's good to be number one at everything."

"流"

The Kanji character for flow.

To discern the flow of time, of eras.

"Being a half step, one step, three steps ahead. Strategizing while constantly predicting what's to come."

"What I'm trying to do is aim for the very center of the very center."

"There's no need to overcomplicate things. Contrarian people who decide purposely to go against the flow of the times have failed as entrepreneurs. Contrarians are not suited for business."

"You have to be selective about who you battle against. You can choose the market you go into, and that's a very important decision."

"The president chooses what business domains the company will go into."

When combined, the characters for "one" and "flow" mean "top-notch."

"攻"

The Kanji character for attack.

"What's bad is not taking on challenges."

"You can't do reasonable things and expect to revolutionize things."

What is "攻" for a entrepreneur?

"Knowing a lot about technologies. Being unmatched in sales and incredible at negotiation."

Son's younger brother Taizo got to the heart of this when he wrote "The Theory of Masayoshi Son."[①]

---

① https://www.facebook.com/taizoson/posts/10153875140629492

"Someone said to me, 'Masayoshi Son seems more like a VC fund partner than the president of a company.' This observation is in some respects totally wrong, but in others totally accurate."

It is a fact that Son has strategized for and implemented numerous large-scale buy-outs, and that he has performed well with regards to his venture capital investments.

On the other hand, however, it is the knowledge that he accrued as an entrepreneur that has made this success possible.

His success, as a businessperson, in constructing Internet infrastructure all throughout Japan, running portal websites, managing E-commerce, and so forth, is what allows him to evaluate companies at the same level as professional investors.

Taizo Son says about Son's abilities, "The fact that he can predict the future, evaluating technologies through both technological and financial perspectives—this is something he's better at than almost everybody in the world. And in that sense, it may not be an exaggeration to say that he's the world's best venture capitalist."

"守"

The Kanji character for defense.

"守" is finance, cash.

"Most start-ups fail because of issues with cash flow."

"Acquire the capital to go on the offense."

"Make sure to keep a healthy cash flow, while also going on the offensive."

"We attack and defend at the same time."

"Complete compliance with laws and regulations. We cannot do anything that goes against justice."

"群"

The Kanji character for group.

Do not rely on "individuals," whether it be one product, one person, or one field of business.

"We try to be heterogenous on purpose."

The objective is to have mutual bonds of companionship, a strategy involving multiple business models.

"You can't go 300 years on a single brand, on a single business model."

Yahoo (current Z Holdings), Alibaba, Arm…Number-one companies that share the same ambition, coming together and coexisting. The SoftBank Group itself is a corporate group that is autonomous, decentralized, and cooperative.

Chapter 5

Talk the Talk, Walk the Walk

I Will Always Honor Our Promise

It was 2005, and Son had just handed Steve Jobs a sketch he had drawn, of an idea he had had. It was of an iPod that also functioned as a cell phone.

"I don't need that, Masa. I have my own."

This was two years before the release of the iPhone, but the vision of what it would be was already complete in Jobs' mind. But Son wasn't discouraged.

"Once your product is complete, give the ones for Japan to me."

Son was proposing that Jobs give him sales rights for the product in Japan, once it was released.

"You're crazy, Masa. I haven't even talked to anyone about development yet," said Jobs, shocked.

"But I'll give it to you because you came to see me first."

"I'll be your Japan carrier, if you honor that promise."

Son went on to buy Vodafone Japan, the Japanese leg of the U.K. company Vodafone, for 15.5 billion dollars in 2006. This was the beginning of what is now the communications company SoftBank.

Of course, they had never signed any contracts. They both knew, however, the verbal agreements between them carried far more weight than any contract.

On October 5, 2011, Jobs passed away at the age of 56. Son immediately released a statement, mourning his death.

"It's very sad. Steve Jobs was a modern genius who was an expert in both art and technology. In several hundred years, people will look back on him as a figure equivalent to Leonardo da Vinci. His achievements will live on forever."

Two years after Jobs' death, on October 21, 2013, Son lost someone who was irreplaceable to him: Kazuhiko Kasai. He was 76.

Kasai had worked his way up the ladder to being the chairman at a major Japanese bank, and become a Director at SoftBank (current SoftBank Group) at the age of 63, at Son's request. He had always supported Son, even during the dot com collapse, when SoftBank's stock price became a hundredth of what it had been before, and even when the ADSL business had lost tens of billions of yen four years in a row. Even when Son had made the dramatic decision to buy out

Vodafone.

There had been just one instance in which Kasai had been in fierce disagreement with Son. It was around the time the chaos from the collapse of Lehman Brothers was finally settling down, and SoftBank's company performance was going up.

Son said, in his condolence address for Kasai, "I personally thought the stock volatility worried investors, and it was tedious to explain these fluctuations to analysts and journalists too. So I said to him, 'I think maybe we should go private, and I can be personally responsible for the company,' and he stopped me, saying, 'I am completely against that idea.'"

Kasai said to Son, "It's true the company is doing very well now, so it would be possible for us to go back to being private—it would be possible to get those resources. We'd figure it out. But is this really what you want? SoftBank needs to go out into the world and, become even bigger. Are you really going to make our dream smaller just because things are tedious, or complicated?"

Looking back on Kasai's words, Son said, "Now, looking back on it, I realize that we probably wouldn't have been able to buy out Sprint if Kasai hadn't stopped me at that point. It would have been impossible for us to have dreamed as big as we did after that, too."

It was then that Son had etched these words into his mind.

"I will honor our promise."

Kasai had always supported Son and his boundless ambitions. This was exactly why he had been so against the idea of Son making this decision that would limit his dream. Son understood that with all of his heart.

A promise is a sharing of an incredible dream. It is also a promise to yourself.

Even now, Son has not forgotten this promise. He will make it happen.

My Hair Isn't Receding. I'm Just Advancing

On January 8, 2013, Son sent a tweet.

"My hair isn't receding. I'm just advancing."

This was in response to a tweet that joked about Son's "dramatically receding" hairline. This response got him over 40,000 retweets, and acclaim, as well as quite a few laughs.

Son was indeed advancing continually. Through a series of large-scale buyouts, he'd accelerated his pace.

In 1995, he bought the sales division of the world's largest computer trade fair, COMDEX, for approximately 80 billion yen, then in 1996, Ziff Davis Publishing, the world's largest publisher for computer-related literature, for approximately 210 billion yen. He had invested a total of approximately 290 billion yen, at a time when SoftBank's (current SoftBank Group) corporate value, following its initial public offering in 1994, was 270 billion yen—less than the amount he had invested. He had listed the company at 36 years old, and made these massive deals over the course of the next two years. Says Son, "I acquired the map and the compass I needed to sally forth into the world."

In 2006, SoftBank aquired out Vodafone Japan (current SoftBank) for approximately 1.75 trillion yen. This acquisition of the telecommunications carrier allowed Son to gain sales right to the iPhone, thereby dramatically increasing the number of contracts for the company. In 2013, he bought out the U.S. telecommunications company Sprint for approximately 1.8 trillion yen. And in 2013, he bought out the major U.K. semiconductor design company Arm for approximately 3.3 trillion yen.

The discussion on balding continued as well, with dramatic developments. Nine months after the "advancing" tweet, on October 8, 2013, Son responded to an article on "the bald and pointless price-cutting war between SoftBank and its competitors." "Not bald yet. There's still a little left," he retweeted. There was another tweet that said, "Balding isn't a disease. It's what it means to be a man."

Shinya Yamanaka, Nobel Laureate in Physiology or Medicine

2012, has also joked about hair. At the Nobel Prize ceremony, Yamanaka, a professor at Kyoto University and director of the university's Center for iPS Cell Research and Application Building, drew laughs with his comment about his co-winner John Gurdon.

"I admire you so much—with regards to everything, including your hair."

"I admire your brilliant head—both inside and outside [your thick hair]."

Son and Yamanaka have more than a few things in common.

Yamanaka's father was the manager of a small-scale factory in town. Like Son, he grew up watching his father, who was self-reliant and made an independent living. He became a doctor, he says, because his father told him he "wasn't suited for management, and shouldn't take on the business." Despite that, Yamanaka is now the director of his research center, and has become a king of sorts with regards to procuring funds through methods like crowdfunding.

Son went to the U.S. at the age of 16 and had experienced the "freeing of the self" that happens under the Californian skies. Yamanaka, after completing his PhD in 1993, studied abroad as a postdoctoral fellow at the University of California, San Francisco's Gladstone Institutes at the age of 30. There, he devoted himself to the research that would serve as the foundation for his later research in iPS cell production. Yamanaka, who said he made a clumsy doctor, found that his skills as a researcher blossomed in this new environment. It seems there is something truly special, magical, about those blue skies in California.

This, however, was not the only thing Yamanaka gained during his time abroad.

VW, or "Vision" and "Work Hard." He learned from his teacher Robert Mahley that these two things were all you needed to succeed, not just as a researcher, but in life. This is still Yamanaka's motto, even now.

Son and Yamanaka are both working toward the realization of their dreams, on the world stage. But this isn't to say that they are always stiff and formal. Both men, on occasion, amuse people with their sense of humor. The laughter that they draw moves people's emotions, and acts as the power with which they change their dreams into reality. And these two very individuals also serve as the President and Vice President of the Masason Foundation.

I Would Rather Be Silicon Valley

March 11, 2014. Son began his interview on the popular American TV talk show with Charlie Rose by discussing his respect for legendary

Japanese entrepreneurs.

"Your heroes were Mr. [Soichiro] Honda and Mr. [Akio] Morita of Sony," said Charlie Rose, who at the time was one of America's most famous TV hosts.

Son turned to address the American public, and said, "Because Mr. Honda of Honda and Mr. Morita of Sony had a passion, a vision, and they were founders of huge brands. Because they were pioneers. They pioneered the automotive industry, they pioneered the electronics industry in Japan, fighting against existing powers without help from the government."

Charlie Rose went in with a curveball question.

"Are you more the financial engineer, who understands how to make a deal, but also understands how to find the companies that you want to make a deal with, rather than being the creative guy?"

By financial engineer, Rose probably meant someone who engineers investments—an investment professional. Son, seeing the irony in this statement, responded with a simple metaphor.

"If Steve [Jobs] is art and technology, I am finance and technology."

"No art," said Charlie Rose, surprised. Perhaps it was rare for entrepreneurs to announce that they were not artists.

"I love art, but I'm not an artist.

To me, what's more important is the Information Revolution—

creating a new lifestyle for mankind.

If I can help bring the Information Revolution to mankind, I don't have to do everything myself. I can use everyone else's talent, and I'll be in charge of the infrastructure. I don't have to create a Ferrari or Honda. I can create a highway for all the other amazing automobiles. I can create the toll gates, the entire ecosystem for the automobile revolution. That's what I'm trying to do. I'm bringing the Information Revolution."

Son had once said that Japan, for all its advancements in Internet technologies, suffered from a relative lack of infrastructure (the "highway").

"So I went in to challenge NTT, which had a 99% market share of the Japanese Information Highway."

Rose asked Son what his negotiating philosophy was.

Son's response was measured and confident.

" I'm looking at the future—not the past, not the present. What we can do in 10 years, in 20 years, if we get more power."

— What excites you?

"The Information Revolution is the only thing I want to devote my life to. Mankind had the Agricultural Revolution, the Industrial Revolution, and now this is the third one—the Information Revolution. This is a significant development, and it'll last for the next 300 years.

That's why we have a 300-year-vision, and why we want to focus on the Information Revolution," Son said.

In the conversation that follows, it becomes clear why Son had announced "I'm not an artist," with such pride. Son also took issue with the zero-sum mindset of many businesses today.

"I don't care whether these technologies are invented by us and our employees," he said. "What I want is to incorporate everybody's innovations into our ecosystem.

"So many American companies are interested in one brand, one business model to conquer the world.

"I'm not that kind of guy. I believe in partnerships, and we do many joint ventures. I make my own decisions about which entrepreneurs to invest in, and try to help them develop their passions. If I can assist all these incredible entrepreneurs, we can come up with great technologies, great services. And nothing would make me more happy.

"I don't need to be a hero. I'd rather be a hero for the total ecosystem that we create. That is my 300-year vision. I don't constrain myself to one product, one business model, one brand."

When the advancement of technology is your number one priority, there is no need to be an artist. Son could use his financial power to support the "artists," the entrepreneurs—to fire up their passions and drive them to success. This is Son's line of thought.

In that sense, Son's stance on entrepreneurship is clearly at odds with companies like Honda Mortor and Sony. This change in perspective may be the most significant innovation Son has brought to the Japanese corporate landscape.

As Son put it, "I would rather be Silicon Valley."

This desire goes far beyond creating a company or a community that could exist in Silicon Valley. The passion with which he spoke conveyed his desire for he himself to be the Silicon Valley ecosystem.

Free Yourself! Fly Free!

On December 5, 2016, Son established the Masason Foundation using his own private funds. For Vice President, he appointed Shinya Yamanaka of Kyoto University, Nobel Laureate in Physiology or Medicine 2012. The directors included such names as Makoto Gonokami, President of The University of Tokyo, and advisors included Yoshiharu Habu, a professional shogi player.

His objective in establishing the foundation was announced as follows.

"Providing an environment that enables youth with high aspirations and exceptional talents to develop their skills, and contributing to the future of humankind."

There's a Japanese dish that Son dislikes called makunouchi bento (the most standard type of Japanese bento, with rice and several different side dishes in a good balance). He even once told his secretary, who was going out to buy him a bento for lunch, "Just not makunouchi bento, please."

It's not that he has very specific taste in food. He just likes it when bento are clear about what they're offering—meat in a meat bento, for example, fish in a fish bento, Chinese food in a Chinese bento, etc. For him, the best case scenario is choosing from amidst multiple, very unique bento. They don't have to be from famous stores. He doesn't care about brands.

Once, when I met with Son, I brought him not a dorayaki[①], but a "torayaki" that I'd bought at a small Japanese confectionery downtown, as a gift. It is called a torayaki because the grill marks make a pattern like tiger (tora) stripes. It is the kind of Japanese confectionary that's made by old couples in a small kitchen, very good but plain and simple, with a distinct characteristic. This is the kind of food that Son likes.

For the celebration of the company's 30th anniversary, I decided to take kohaku manju (red and white steamed buns, thought to be

---

① Dorayaki: A Japanese confectionary, with two discshaped, pancake-like patties (made with flour, eggs, sugar, etc.) sandwiching sweet red bean jam auspicious) instead of torayaki. I asked them to inscribe the number 30 on the buns. When I received it, however, I was stunned. Perhaps they had never made a commemorative product with an inscription on it—but the way the numbers were inscribed looked rough, inexperienced. Son, however, enjoyed this fact immensely. It tasted good, but the inscription was obviously not done well. He gazed at the manju, as if to relish in this clumsiness, and thanked me very politely, as he always did.

His felt similarly towards people as well.

The Masason Foundation supports young people with exceptional talents. As of July 11, 2019, the foundation is supporting 187 young people, with ages as varied as 8 to 28. It gathers those with exceptional talents in a variety of fields, from robotics, programming, mathematics, physics, and science, to literature and even art.

On December 26, 2018, at the Masason Foundation Annual Report Meeting, Son gave these young people a pep talk.

"I went to the U.S. when I was 16, and was very inspired by what I saw there. The environment was completely different. Interacting with people who think differently, in a different language, really activates your entire brain. And as you young people, with all of your exceptional talents, spend your days together, you will inspire each other and drive one another to be even better. Keep your eyes open, create big opportunities for yourself, and grow into adults who will be of use to people."

What he is doing is creating a place where people with exceptional talents can all mingle with one another, and co-create.

"Japanese education focuses on bringing everyone up to the 'average' level. The U.S. and China, on the other hand, are moving towards a system that focuses on bringing out and enhancing the unique talents of people at the very top. My work is to assist in cultivating these exceptional talents that will be essential to the future growth of Japan, who will be Japan's future leaders," said Son.

When Son was in elementary school, his dream was to become a teacher. At the time, however, he had given up on this dream due to certain issues, including his nationality.

After a Masason Foundation event on February 10, 2017, I asked Son…

What is his message to young people?

"'Free yourself! Fly free!' This, in a lot of different ways. This is what I would want to tell them."

Son watches over the future of these exceptionally talents, eyes shining.

Chapter 6

Theory of Technological Evolution

Read the Tides

It was February 6, 2019, at the third quarter earnings results briefing for FY 2018, and Son was discussing his vision.

"When I say vision, you may think of something romantic, like a dream or a fantasy—something vague and indistinct."

That's not how Son thinks about it.

"For me personally, a vision is a challenge you take on, something that's very clear, very logical, and very certain."

But in order to make your vision clear and substantial, it's essential to have a clear and accurate understanding of the times, and how they're changing.

Son invited the audience to "look back on the SoftBank Group's 40-year history." Since its establishment, he announced, there is one thing that the company has done every single day, and that they will continue to do. This something is "driving the Information Revolution."

"The waves of the Information Revolution come every decade or so, causing gradual paradigm shifts. The Information Revolution is a massive revolution, the kind that happens only once every several hundred years. And within this revolution, there are forward-moving phases about once every 10 years."

He looked back on the history of the Information Revolution, dividing it into phases and explaining it to the audience. First, he said, "There was the age of large-scale computers, and then the personal computer was born. PCs were born, and then SoftBank was born. Then came the Internet, then broadband, then smartphones, with progressions that created paradigm shifts happening about once every 10 years. And right now, I believe we're facing the largest paradigm shift—the AI revolution. I believe the AI revolution will be the greatest paradigm shift within the Information Revolution."

Though Son believes that a vision should be very clear, logical, and certain, he also understands that "vision isn't something that comes to you all of a sudden." He says, "It's something you have to think about on a daily basis, all the time, until your mind is completely wrung out—it's not something that just pops into your head after two, three days of thinking."

Put another way, a vision that accurately captures the shifting times shouldn't be fuzzy. Yet it requires endlessly long, deep thought to grasp those shifts in an unequivocal way.

There is something that Son always says, at the very beginning, to any young start-up founder he meets from any country.

"Read the changing of the times, then read beyond it. Challenge yourself to something that's a half-step, a whole step, a whole three steps ahead of the times, and wait there."

"Place the axis of your business in a growing industry, not a sinking one."

"Read the tides."

Read the tides, and you'll begin to see.

"The more unsure you are, the farther ahead you need to look."

Looking for the Next Jack Ma

The SoftBank Academia special lecture in October 2015 was held as a dialogue between Son and Nikesh Arora (Representative Director, President of SoftBank Group at the time). Academia is a project that aims to cultivate entrepreneurs of the upcoming generation, including Son's successor.

Nikesh marveled at the fact that the SoftBank Group looks for young start-up founders and invests in their passion and creativity every year, and that it does so as a business strategy.

Nikesh also predicted that "five to ten of these entrepreneurs will be the next Elon Musk, Steve Jobs, or Larry Page. So the SoftBank Group will become the portfolio of entrepreneurs."

As entrepreneurs from previous generations mature, the SoftBank Group brings start-up founders from younger generations into its portfolio. SoftBank makes it possible to provide money and resources to the younger generation. It also provides a "family" network of companies and other start-up founders that can support them, as well as mentorship and lessons on entrepreneurship. This is exactly what Son did with Jack Ma, said Nikesh.

Passionately. He went on to ask Son, "How do you find these people? What are the criteria, when there are so many companies in the world? The last time I checked, I found there were 1.5 million companies in the start-up phase. Yet you still managed to find Jack Ma. How do you find these people for the SoftBank family?"

The question was one that every start-up founder in the world would want to know the answer to.

Son replied, "Yes, we have to create some kind of system [to do that]."

Son does not want to rely on personal judgment for this task. Instead, he wants to create a system that allows the organization itself to discover promising start-up founders.

"We need to have some kind of system to identify the more exciting companies, exciting founders, among all the early-stage start-ups. We also need to have some kind of system to screen these start-up founders. We screen them to see if they're big enough fish, and let go of the small fish. When the remaining fish get bigger, we have to decide which company we should or should not invest in."

A famous story about Son relays how, in 1999, he made the decision to invest 20 million dollars in Jack Ma "lightning-quick, in five minutes." Son later commented, "I looked into his eyes, and felt we were the same kind of person."

This is probably not the whole story, however. Son does not speak much about his inner thoughts. It's entirely possible that he had been prepared, that he had already done thorough research and analysis, and had developed his own system for discovering such entrepreneurs before that fateful moment in 1999.

Sensors, Trilobites, and the Cambrian Explosion

It was October 2016, and Arm's annual TechCon conference was under way in San Jose, California, in the heart of Silicon Valley. This was soon after the SoftBank Group's acquisition of Arm, a major UK semiconductor design company—a global entity with an incredible array of intellectual assets. Son asked the crowd.

"What was the first species on this earth to have eyes?"

He paused for a moment, then went on.

"It was the trilobite."

His point?

The eyes are the ultimate sensors. Look back on the origin of all living creatures, and you will notice that the appearance of the trilobite, with its eye "sensors," immediately preceded the birth and evolution of all kinds of different creatures. This, Son says, is a lesson for us in modern society as well.

"Nowadays, we can install the latest technologies into our IoT. With this latest technology, you can put sensors onto IoT, get them to undergo recognition and deep learning, make deductions, and actuate them. This cycle is the same as the evolution of animal species. In that way, the Cambrian explosion and IoT explosion are essentially the same thing."

What he means is that the trilobite of the IoT era has just now come into existence.

Many kinds of IoT equipment, made with the latest technologies, now come with sensors. So many things now have eyes.

Sensors make it possible to "recognize" all of creation. One of Son's favorite theories is that deduction, based in recognition, is what has allowed humanity to evolve to this extent. For instance, how human beings were able to "recognize" birds flying in the sky, and deduce and ultimately create the shape and structure of a machine that would allow for flight.

Big data and deep learning will allow various sensor-equipped objects to recognize and make deductions about the enormous array of phenomena captured with their "eyes."

And thus the inorganic begins its evolution like a living creature.

This is Son's vision of the future.

Looking Forward to the Singularity

Nowadays, computers have become far smarter than humans at things like chess, go, and weather reports. And 30 years from now, they will be even smarter. This is something that we, mankind, have just begun to accept as our new reality.

October 1, 2017. Son was on investor David Rubenstein's TV show, when he proposed a theory and some facts that seemed to fly in the face of this belief.

Son's English speeches, like his Japanese ones, are straightforward, and cover only essential points. "Arm has a 99% market share," he began.

Arm, which SoftBank Group acquired in 2016, has near complete control of the design of mobile microprocessors, which are considered to be the "brain" of the computer.

"In 20 years, they are going to ship 1 trillion chips, design 1 trillion chips. Nobody on this planet can live without these chips. They're anywhere—in the car, in the refrigerator, everywhere. If these chips are something that everybody needs, and there's one company that has a 99% market share, that's a valuable thing."

There are those, however, who feel threatened by this value—more specifically, the idea that robots will become so smart that they will wipe out mankind entirely. David Rubenstein asked Son about this fear.

"There is that risk," Son admitted, before moving the discussion to a more optimistic note.

"But if you look at the history of mankind, people were killing each other with countless battles. But today, we don't have that kind of thing in our everyday lives. We are more civilized. So when we get to a point where robotic superintelligence far exceeds mankind's intelligence, we'll understand that fighting is not a good thing—that harmony is better in general and for society."

Son believes this from the bottom of his heart.

"Robots think about us, they help us. They'll make us happier, so we have more room to love one another."

Asked "What gives you the greatest pleasure in the world?" Son's responded, "I have a clear vision for the singularity that is quickly approaching."

He derives great pleasure, he says, from thinking about how he and his portfolio companies can help mankind build a better world. How singularity may allow people to live better in the future by eliminating accidents and illnesses, and protecting people from sadness. How he can work with others towards this dream. Son believes that solving these issues would benefit mankind, which is why he is so excited for the singularity to arrive.

Son's words are clear and forceful.

"There's still lots of efforts to be made. But unique efforts like this create a lot of opportunity. Difficulties, in that sense, can be an advantage. This is definitely an exciting life, and I'm having fun."

Chapter 7

To All Those Who Will Live with AI

Like Young Jedi Knights

March 2019. Son was being interviewed by David Faber, who asked him, "Don't you think you have the ability to influence significantly where technology is going?"

"I'm excited to be a part of it," Son said, rebutting the claim.

"Things are happening without me."

"But still," he continued passionately, "I would like to support start-up founders who have dreams and passions. Technology is evolving very quickly. So if I can be a good facilitator or supporter, I will be very excited to do so."

According to Son, there have been three significant changes in the industrial sector in the past 30 years.

The first is the increase in the number of transistors in CPUs (central processing units). The second is increased memory capacity. And the third is increased communication speeds.

The first two are a million times what they used to be, and the third three million times more.

This has enormous impacts on technology and our lifestyles. If these elements continue to evolve, a CPU with a million times more power will be equipped with a memory capacity a million times of what it was before, and will be able to communicates at three million times the speed. This is expected to bring extraordinary change.

The power of computers has made AI (artificial intelligence) a reality. And the power of AIs to process vast amounts of data and make predictions has made it possible for us to realize a future where robots are equipped with intelligence.

As Son went on, discussing his dream for the future, Faber—always the journalist—remarked, "That's been a focus of yours, I know, in terms of where you're investing."

By that he meant that it made financial sense for Son, who was investing in AI, to talk about his dreams for AI. Faber went on, "I think you've said AI will be the biggest revolution in human history."

"Yes."

——Bigger than anything we've seen?

"Much, much bigger."

——You've said that you want SoftBank (Group) to be the company that makes the most contribution to human evolution.

"Yes."

——Do you believe you can actually fulfill that?

"I would like to make it happen."

——How?

"By empowering the new forces that come in. These new, young start-up founders, in my view, they are Jedi [from the Star Wars series]."

Son believes that young people who jump straight into the world of start-ups after university are "like young Jedi knights."

"These young Jedi are learning how to fly. And some of them are already flying, in fact. It's fun to watch our young Jedi creating new lifestyles and solving many of the issues that mankind still faces."

In Son's vision, these young Jedi knights will come up with cures for incurable diseases, reduce the occurrence of accidents, and in general help eliminate the inefficiency, suffering, and sadness in the world today.

Son is well aware, however, that many of these young Jedi knights will struggle, and sometimes fail during their journeys. It is not an easy thing to start a company and accomplish something. Son, however, must also see beyond that, to a future where they—even wounded or suffering—stand up again and return to the battle even stronger than before.

AI Will Redefine All Industries

It was February 6, 2019, and Son was speaking at the SoftBank Group Earnings Results Briefing for the third quarter of the FY2018. He was discussing the AI revolution.

First, he told the audience about the current reality.

"10 years ago, only one of the top ten companies in the world was an Internet company—just one. And now, in just 10 years, Internet companies make up seven of the top ten."

Looking at the world market cap rankings, and Microsoft was the only tech company in the top ten in 2009. Fast forward to 2019, and Apple leads the same rankings, alongside seven other U.S. and Chinese Internet companies.

In other words, the Internet had brought on a paradigm shift. This is what the Information Revolution has done thus far.

Son predicts, however, that the future of the Information Revolution will see AI taking center stage. "In several years, more than half the top ten companies in the world are going to be AI companies," he said. Why?

"These Internet companies that make up seven of the world's top ten companies—what industries, specifically, did they redefine?" Son asked.

"In simple terms, just two. The advertisement industry and the retail industry. The Internet redefined these two industries."

Facebook and Google redefined the business model for the advertisement industry, stealing customers from traditional forms of media. Amazon and Alibaba redefined the retail industry with E-commerce, stealing customers from traditional forms of retail.

The paradigm shift that will happen as a result of AI, however, will have much broader effects than that brought on by the Internet to date. AI will redefine power relationships across the automobile industry, of course, but also all kinds of other industries, from transportation to education, medicine, real estate, finance, and more.

Son predicts that "AI will redefine all sorts of industries."

Son repeated the core point of his theory. In the past 30 years, the number of transistors in CPUs, memory capacity, and communication speeds have increased. The first two are a million times what they used to be, and the third three million times more. In the next 30 years, he declared, there will be further increase in these numbers.

"For the first time in the history of humanity, human beings have succeeded in creating AI that works better than our own brain cells. These forms of AI are self-learning. Instead of human beings teaching them what they need to know, they sense data on their own from a wide array of inputs, including IoT, mobile devices, cars, and buildings, etc., and use this data to make their deductions, drawing conclusions from the data itself. They will redefine so many industries. This is my vision of the future."

Son is optimistic about the evolution of humankind, and he uses simple, fitting analogies to describe it.

"Humankind saw birds flying high in the sky, and thought, how great would it be to be able to fly through the sky, and so Leonardo da Vinci created a prototype for the plane."

"Copernicus looked up at the stars in the sky and thought, maybe it's not the sky that's moving, maybe it's the earth we're standing on that's moving, and so he proposed the heliocentric system, and changed the way people thought of things from the bottom up."

"Einstein saw light and proposed $E=mc^2$, the theory of relativity."

"In other words, humankind has evolved through deductions from what we can see and feel."

Son thinks that "deduction is the greatest source of humankind's evolution."

In the AI revolution, AI will process this same kind of data—data that we can see and touch—and make deductions, with greater and greater computing power. This is the reason that the AI revolution will bring such significant advancements for humankind.

Son is confident in his assessment.

"AI will redefine all industries. And this AI revolution has only just begun."

Deviations, Delayed Reactions

On February 6, 2019, at SoftBank Group's Earnings Results Briefing, Son proclaimed, "I think in a few dozen years, 5th Avenue in New York will be filled with AI-controlled, self-driving cars." Just as, he said, how horse-drawn carriages going to and fro on 5th Avenue in the past had transformed into automobiles over the course of a few dozen years.

As for the "few dozen years," he clarified, "This could move five years forwards or backwards, give or take."

"But I personally would say that five, ten years is just a deviation. It's the general direction that's important."

From horse-drawn carriages to automobiles. And another overarching paradigm shift, from cars driven by human beings to cars driven by AI.

Why? Because AI-driven cars cause fewer accidents than human-driven ones. And the three elements required in computing—namely the number of transistors in CPUs, memory capacity, and communication speed—are still very much evolving, even now.

He has a vision, and a logical explanation for this vision.

"Anything else is just a deviation."

He likes that word—deviation.

On this day, Son showed a formula on-screen. It said, "25-4=9?"

"The shareholder value of SoftBank Group, as a pure holding company, is the equity value of our holdings, 25 trillion yen, minus SoftBank Group's net debt, 4 trillion, so 21 trillion yen. There's a huge discrepancy between this number and the current market cap of its holding company, SoftBank Group Corp., which is approximately 9 trillion yen."[1]

When asked by a reporter how this "discrepancy" could be improved, he answered instantly.

"It's just delayed reaction. That's it. Time will be the judge."

Some have said that the SoftBank Group's corporate value should be cut, since the group takes so many risks and carries a lot of debt.

"But all of this will go away with time, and there will be no more noise."

Son mentioned the companies that Warren Buffett—also known

---

[1] The "equity value of the SoftBank Group's holdings," is as of February 6, 2019, the "SoftBank Group's net debt" is as of the end of 2018, and the "market cap of SoftBank Group Corp." is as of February 6, 2019.

as the Oracle of Omaha—had invested in, and how the valuations measured by "sum-of-the-parts" of these companies now came with a premium instead of a discount.

"There's always a delayed reaction to things that move quickly. I am always moving forward," he said, then added jokingly, without missing a beat, "Although everyone laughed at me for saying, 'My hair isn't receding, I'm just advancing.'"

He smiled slightly, then said clearly, "I think people's evaluation of the group will catch up in time."

Deviations, delayed reactions. That's all.

"Big Talk" Mentality

"What's missing in Japan right now is that *obora* mentality."

The term "obora" in Japanese has a negative connotation, and in English would be the equivalent to "braggart," or "big talk." Son's translation, however, is different.

"In English, it would be 'big vision.'"

It was May 9, 2019, at the SoftBank Group's Earnings Results Briefing for FY2018, and Son had announced that they would begin preparations for establishing SoftBank Vision Fund 2.

The Vision Fund makes concentrated investments in leading

companies that utilize AI. The companies to receive these investments are the world's elite, including ride-share companies Uber and DiDi, which have found success in the U.S. and China respectively, India-born hotel chain OYO, and more. Many of them are unicorn companies (start-ups with a valuation of 1 billion dollars or more). Son is a "self-proclaimed unicorn hunter."

Currently, this fund—which has devoted itself to the future of AI—is considered "the number one greatest source of growth" for the SoftBank Group, with Son declaring his grand ambition to get the Group's total market cap up to 200 trillion yen by 2040, at the general stockholder meeting on June 29.

There are some who mock this kind of ambition, who will call it "big talk (obora)."

"The Vision Fund is a bubble." "He's devoting too much to unrealized profit that may never be realized." "That's too much interest-bearing debt."

Son brushesd off these kinds of criticisms as background noise.

"When I was a kid, I liked to fish. I'd set up a net and catch a whole bunch." In the Internet revolution that came before this AI revolution, he had missed countless opportunities for investment. Looking back, he says it was because he didn't have enough funds. "This time," he says, "I'll get them all—no excuses."

And so Son goes on with his "big talk," and his big numbers.

"Let's say SoftBank Group's investment is 6 trillion yen[①]. If the fund has an annual growth of 35%, in ten years it will be 20 times the original amount. With a more conservative estimate—an annual growth of 26%—for the ten years after that, it'll be 10 times the amount after ten years, and 200 times the amount after 20 years. Even with all-around more conservative estimates, an annual growth of 19% after 20 years would bring us to 33 times the original amount, with 6 trillion yen becoming 200 trillion yen."

"We want to start counting in trillions," he had said once, as to his dream. Who knew it would be 200 trillion?

At the 2019 annual shareholders meeting, SoftBank played a video from a shareholders general meeting 15 years earlier. In that video, Son, still in his mid-40s, said, "We want to be able to make one, two trillion yen in profits by the time I'm in my 60s." Then, without missing a beat, he quipped, "Whoops, is that 'big talk'?" inviting laughter from the audience. He was speaking at a time when the company had been over 10 billion yen in the red for four years in a row. It might have been "big talk," but even then, he was honest about what he wanted.

And at this FY 2018, Son is 61 years old, and SoftBank Group has

---

① As of the end of September 2019, the SoftBank Group's commitment to the Vision Fund was a total of 33.1 billion dollars (approximately 3.5 trillion yen).

made over 1 trillion yen in net profit.

What Son is really saying is that his "big talk" is actually a "big vision," one that he is capable of realizing.

I Might Have Regrets, But I Won't Shrink Away

November 6, 2019. At SoftBank Group's FY2019 Mid-Term Earning Results Briefing, people were reeling from "WeWork shock."

SoftBank Group reported approximately 700 billion yen in net losses—the most ever for the company on a quarterly basis. One of the biggest contributors to this result was The We Company, which offers the coworking service WeWork. The loss stemmed largely from the decline in the fair value of The We Company, which both the SoftBank Vision Fund and the SoftBank Group had invested in, the latter through its subsidiary.

Reporters' questions focused mainly on this issue.

In a dramatic shift from Son's stance five months ago, when he reiterated his vast ambition to "raise market cap to 200 trillion yen in 20 years," the Mid-Term briefing found him saying, again and again, "I regret my decisions." He apologized for the concern he had caused for shareholders, financial institutions, and investors, as well as their many affiliates. He promised to learn from his mistakes, and work towards better management.

What "regrets" did Son have, and what had he learned?

His first regret was that SoftBank had overestimated WeWork's value. In October, SoftBank Group announced a financial package for WeWork that included an acceleration of existing warrants for an average acquisition cost that was about a quarter of prior investment costs.

Son's second regret was being too lax in the governance of the companies the SoftBank Group had invested in. For instance, at the time WeWork sought to go pubic, its board of directors had approved the provision of "super-voting" stocks (with 20 times the voting rights of regular stocks) to WeWork's founder. The SoftBank Group had had one member on the nine-member board of directors, and was unable to prevent board decisions at a company controlled by the founder.

Going forward, the SoftBank Group would strengthen its relationship with WeWork by having five members in the ten-member board of directors. The company also planned to create guidelines for other portfolio companies and future investments, and scrutinize their governance.

On this day, Son calmly explained SoftBank Group's mistakes, and the measures the company would take to rectify them.

His expression clouded over, however, when he was asked about WeWork founder Adam Neumann.

"I think he is someone who has good parts and bad parts. I think I probably overvalued his good parts. He's very brilliant in terms of how motivated, how aggressive, how artistic he is. I may have been so taken by those aspects that I was blind to the negatives. I very much regret my evaluation of him in that sense."

At heart, Son believes that human nature is fundamentally good. This isn't the first time he has been burned because of it. But when it happens, he learns from his mistakes and looks to the future.

Some veteran journalists commented that Son may have lost some of his powers of insight with age.

Perhaps in response, Son emphasized the fact that the SoftBank Group would reevaluate the methods used to make decisions on Vision Fund investments.

The key factor would be free cash flow.

Tech companies, including GAFA (Google, Apple, Facebook, Amazon) are always operating in the red in the early stages after establishment. It takes several years for such businesses to gain momentum.

But if you are able to estimate how much cash flow a company would generate several years down the road once it has taken off, you could calculate its appropriate present value.

What Son was saying, in other words, was that it isn't just romanticized views of founders that drives him to invest in companies.

"I regret my actions," Son said, again and again, but his ambition with the Vision Fund hasn't waned whatsover.

Proudly, he stated two facts.

The first was that the SoftBank Group's shareholder value had increased by over 1.4 trillion yen since the 1st Quarter Earning Results Briefing three months earlier. Their equity value of holdings had increased by a total of 2.1 trillion yen. The shareholder value, which is derived by subtracting the net debt from the equity values of holdings, is the management index that Son most cares about—and this had climbed to 22.4 trillion yen.

Son's second point was that the Vision Fund's cumulative investment performance was positive. As of the end of September 2019, the net unrealized gain of the fund was 1.3 trillion yen, and the net realized gain 500 billion yen, for a total of 1.8 trillion yen in increased value. Their unrealized loss, on the other hand, was 600 billion yen.

"The Vision Fund, as of right now, is 3:1 in wins-losses, when you look at amounts."

"In either case, it's impossible to win 10:0 [when investing in start-ups]."

"[The WeWork shock] is not a storm. It's just a ripple."

"There's no abnormality in the system. The vision and the strategy haven't changed. The decision I've made, the policy I'm going to follow, is to keep moving resolutely forward."

This wasn't just Son putting on a brave face.

One thing he said seemed to embody the entrepreneurial spirit in particular: "I might have regrets, but I won't shrink away."

Failure is a given when you are attempting new things. It's about what you learn from them—what you do after. That's where you will find true value.

Be Crazy About Something!

It was April 2019, at the SoftBank Career Live, and Son was speaking in front of an audience of young people who were about to take on the world in their first jobs.

"First, a word about living in this era, where the world is changing so drastically. My advice to you is to 'be crazy about something.'"

Crazy—a strong word. With that he began his explanation, addressing the everyday lives of his young audience.

"Have you ever been crazy about something in your life? Maybe you were crazy about sports, music, club activities, or all kinds of things. But as you become a working adult, and you start a career that you'll devote most of your life to, I think the greatest life you can live is one in which you can be crazy about your work. That's my belief."

As he spoke, Son must have been looking back at his time as a student, at the moment when he was stirred to tears by the beauty of a computer chip in a magazine photograph under the wide-open blue California sky. He had carefully cut out that page of the magazine, which he'd bought in the supermarket, and stored it safely in a file folder. In that moment of "craziness," he had decided that his life's theme would be the Information Revolution.

"Craziness you'd devote your life to, craziness that's worth devoting your life to. Think to yourself, why am I so crazy about this theme? If you're able to figure this out while you're young, while you're still of this generation, it will be a vital decision for the rest of your life. Choose the mountain you want to climb, and that's half your life already decided for you."

Be crazy about something, and it determines the mountain you'll climb. And anyone, once they've decided on climbing a mountain, will aim for the summit. But this is an extremely difficult task—hard enough if your summit is to be number one in Japan, but even harder if it's number one in the world.

The question is whether you can get to that summit before you die.

Son told his audience that it's the decisions you make when you're young that are important.

"Winning a gold medal at the Olympics, now that's a very hard thing to do. You start training at two, three years old, to win a gold medal in table tennis, and when you turn 18, all of a sudden change your mind and say, you know what, I actually want to do tennis. But when you start playing tennis at 18 years old, winning a gold medal in tennis is borderline impossible. It'd be like going back down a mountain after going up halfway, and then going up a whole new mountain. That's a hard thing, and you'll lose half of your life that way."

There is a limit to how long your life can be. As he went on, Son's words took on more passion.

"It is so important to figure out what theme you're crazy about, what you want to devote your life to pursuing. I was lucky to come across that photo of the computer chip when I was a student, and decide on this one mountain. I lost myself in the work, and even now, my passion for it is still growing. I'm a very happy person."

Who knows which of Son's listeners will take his words to heart?

Afterword

The late Goro Hashimoto, a dear friend of mine and the former Executive Director & Publishing General Manager at SOFTBANK Corp. Japan (current SoftBank Group Corp.), once said, "Son is a digital person with an analog heart."

As a young man, Son achieved great success by founding a company while studying in the U.S. Later, however, he decided to sell it and return to Japan. Why?

When he set out alone to the U.S. at the age of 16, his mother had cried with worry. He promised his mother at that moment that he would return to Japan after his studies were over. And so he returned, to honor his promise. And he started up a company in Japan.

The entrepreneur Masayoshi Son has a strong desire, a conviction, to make people happier through the Information Revolution. I still have my notes from my first interview with Son back in 1987, which spanned five hours. For the 32 years that I've been interviewing Son, his conviction about technological evolution has not wavered in any way.

In writing this book, I first want to thank Masayoshi Son, Chairman and CEO of SoftBank Group Corp. Over the 30 years that I have spent as his interviewer, he has not broken a single promise to me.

In the interview in the prologue, I had the privilege of hearing his passionate thoughts about start-up founders.

"You have to always be thinking about your idea, and thinking hard about it, whether asleep or awake. You have to be so passionate about it that you're basically going to sleep cradling those thoughts, or else it's going to be difficult for you to get too far ahead of everyone else."

"Without that emotional investment, that aspiration, that crazed effort, you won't get anywhere close to growing wings."

I was extremely fortunate in writing this book to be able to speak to Taizo Son, Son's younger brother, who is himself a start-up founder, and who established the company Mistletoe, which invests in start-ups and helps cultivate human resources. He understands the entrepreneur Masayoshi Son better than anybody else.

"The fact that he can predict the future, evaluating technologies through both technological and financial perspectives—this is something he's better at than almost everybody in the world."

"And in that sense, it may not be an exaggeration to say that he's the world's best venture capitalist."

Taizo's "The Theory of Masayoshi Son," which he posted on Facebook, truly got to the heart of who Son is.

I would also like to thank my father-in-law, Shinkichi Sanada.

He pored through the "Pocket Computer Library" (1981) and "Program Library" (1982) texts published by SOFTBANK Corp. Japan (current SoftBank Group Corp.) in their early years, and managed to write a functional program based on the information in these texts. He provided me with this very precious reference material for the writing of this book.

Finally, I would like to thank Masato Hoppo, Editor-in-Chief of Nikkei Top Leader Editorial Department, and Tazu Ono, Deputy Editor-in-Chief and the editor of this book, for their support in my endeavor.

Atsuo Inoue

November 2019

Chronological History (Abridged)

	Masayoshi Son / SoftBank Group	Society / Economics
1957	August 11: Masayoshi Son is born in Tosu City, Saga Prefecture to father Mitsunori and mother Tamako Lee. Decides as a child that he wants to be an entrepreneur, partly due to the influence of his father, who ran multiple businesses	
1964 (7 years old)		The 1964 Summer Olympic Games are held in Tokyo
1973 (16 years old)	April: Enters Kurume University Senior High School in Kurume City, Fukuoka Prefecture Visits the University of California, Berkeley as part of a language training program in the U.S. over the summer Drops out of Kurume University Senior High School in fall	The Paris Peace Accords are signed, and President Richard Nixon declares an end to the Vietnam War. Battles, however, continued for two years after this declaration
1974 (17 years old)	February: Moves to the U.S. September: After studying at a language school, Son transfers into Serramonte High School in Daly City, California in the U.S. as a 2nd-year	
1975 (18 years old)	September: Begins attending Holy Names University	Bill Gates drops out of Harvard University, establishes Microsoft with Paul Allen

	Masayoshi Son / SoftBank Group	Society / Economics
1976 (19 years old)	Sets up his "50-Year Life Plan"	Steve Jobs establishes Apple Computer with Steve Wozniak
1977 (20 years old)	Transfers into the University of California, Berkeley College of Letters and Science as a 3rd-year (major in economics)	
1978 (21 years old)	Establishes M SPEECH SYSTEM INC. in the U.S. Takes time off from school, and returns temporarily to Japan. Sells his invention, an electronic translator with a voice function, to the major electrical appliance manufacturer Sharp, and signs a contract that earns him a million dollars. Marries Masami Ohno, her concentration was on astrophysics at the University of California, Berkeley	
1979 (22 years old)		The Second Oil Shock occurs as a result of the Iranian Revolution and a variety of other factors
1980 (23 years old)	Graduates from the University of California, Berkeley, and returns to Japan	
1981 (24 years old)	March: Establishes Unison World, a planning company, in Fukuoka City. September: Establishes SOFTBANK Corp. Japan (current SoftBank Group Corp.) in Chiyoda Ward, Tokyo, and starts a logistics business for packaged software. Publishes the "Pocket Computer Library"	

	Masayoshi Son / SoftBank Group	Society / Economics
1982 (25 years old)	Begins publication of "Oh! PC" and "Oh! MZ," monthly professional magazines that introduce readers to PCs, software, etc., and starts publishing business	
1983 (26 years old)	Hospitalized for hepatitis, and begins undergoing serious treatment	
1984 (27 years old)	Cured of hepatitis, and is discharged from hospital	Apple Computer, led by Steve Jobs, begins sales of the first generation Macintosh computer
1985 (28 years old)		Steve Jobs removed from command at Apple Computer
1986 (29 years old)	Officially reinstates as Chairman & CEO of company	
1989 (32 years old)		The Berlin Wall comes down Japanese era changes from Showa to Heisei
1990 (33 years old)	July: Changes company name from Softbank Corp. Japan to SoftBank Corp.	The Ministry of Finance Banking Bureau in Japan sends out a notification for total volume control of property-related financing. The Japanese "bubble economy" heads toward collapse
1994 (37 years old)	July: Registeres with Japan Securities Dealers Association	

	Masayoshi Son / SoftBank Group	Society / Economics
1995 (38 years old)	April: Acquires interests in Technology Events Division of the Interface Group in the U.S., which was operating COMDEX, the world's largest PC fair	Microsoft releases Windows 95
1996 (39 years old)	January: Establishes the Yahoo Japan Corporation (current Z Holdings Corporation) through joint investment with Yahoo Inc. in the U.S. February: Acquires Ziff-Davis Publishing Company, U.S. publisher of PC WEEK magazine, provider of leading-edge information on the PC industry, through SoftBank Holdings Inc.	Steve Jobs reinstated at Apple Computer
1998 (41 years old)	January: SoftBank is listed on the First Section of Tokyo Stock Exchange	
1999 (42 years old)	October: Converts to a pure holding company	
2000 (43 years old)	January: Invests in Alibaba	
2001 (44 years old)	September: BB Technologies Corporation (current SoftBank) launches Yahoo! BB comprehensive broadband service	The September 11 (9/11) Attacks occur The Dotcom Bubble bursts
2003 (46 years old)	January: Merges BB Technologies Corporation and three other subsidiaries to form SoftBank BB Corp. (current SoftBank)	
2004 (47 years old)	July: Acquires shares of JAPAN TELECOM CO., LTD (current SoftBank), and entered fixed-line telecommunications business	

	Masayoshi Son / SoftBank Group	Society / Economics
2005 (48 years old)	January: Acquires shares of Fukuoka Daiei Hawks Corp. (current Fukuoka SoftBank HAWKS)	
2006 (49 years old)	April: Acquires shares of U.K.- based Vodafone Group Plc's Vodafone K.K. (current SoftBank) through public tender offer and enters the mobile communications business	
2008 (51 years old)	July: SoftBank Mobile Corp. (current SoftBank) begins sale of iPhone 3G	The U.S. company Lehman Brothers Holding Inc. files for bankruptcy (Lehman Crisis)
2010 (53 years old)	July: Launches SoftBank Academia	
2011 (54 years old)	April: Makes announcement regarding donations/support funds for the Great East Japan Earthquake (1 billion yen from the SoftBank Group, 10 billion yen from Son himself) June: Establishes The Great East Japan Earthquake Recovery Initiatives Foundation July: Establishes Renewable Energy Council, GDC Renewable Energy Council August: Establishes The Renewable Energy Institute October: Establishes SB Energy Corp.	The Great East Japan Earthquake occurs
2013 (56 years old)	July: Completion of Acquisition of U.S.-based Sprint Nextel Corporation (current Sprint)	

	Masayoshi Son / SoftBank Group	Society / Economics
2014 (57 years old)	June: SoftBank Mobile Corp. (current SoftBank) and ALDEBARAN ROBOTICS SAS (current SoftBank Robotics Europe) announces "Pepper", the world's first personal robot that reads emotions	
2015 (58 years old)	April: SoftBank Mobile Corp. (currently SoftBank Corp.), SoftBank BB Corp., SoftBank Telecom Corp. and Ymobile Corporation merges July: Company name of SoftBank Corp. changes to SoftBank Group Corp., and company name of SoftBank Mobile Corp. changes to SoftBank Corp.	
2016 (59 years old)	September: Acquires U.K.-based ARM Holdings Plc (current Arm Limited) December: Establishes the Masason Foundation	The U.K. makes the decision to leave the EU through a referendum
2017 (60 years old)	May: The SoftBank Vision Fund announces its first major closing	Donald Trump is elected as the 45th U.S. President
2018 (61 years old)	April: U.S- based Sprint and T-Mobile US enters into a definitive agreement to merge December: SoftBank is listed on the First Section of Tokyo Stock Exchange	
2019 (62 years old)	February: MONET Technologies joint venture formed by Toyota and SoftBank Corp., started business	Japanese era changes from Heisei to Reiwa The Fukuoka SoftBank HAWKS wins the Japan Series (professional baseball) for the third consecutive time

参考文献

『志高く　孫正義正伝　新版』井上篤夫（実業之日本社文庫）

『とことん　孫正義物語』井上篤夫（フレーベル館）

『事を成す　孫正義の新30年ビジョン』井上篤夫（実業之日本社）

『孫家の遺伝子』孫泰蔵（角川書店）

『僕たちがスタートアップした理由』MOVIDA JAPAN 株式会社 Seed Acceleration Div. 著／孫泰蔵監修（フォレスト出版）

『つまらなくない未来』小島健志著／孫泰蔵監修（ダイヤモンド社）

「プレジデント」1997年1月号（プレジデント社）

「リーダーが『座右』に置く孫子の『名言』」

「日経トップリーダー」2017年1月号（日経BP）

「『経営者』になった『山中伸弥』町工場の後は継がなかったけれども」